• HALSGROVE DISCOVER SERIES ➤

STONEHENGE and AVEBURY

THE WORLD HERITAGE SITE

• HALSGROVE DISCOVER SERIES ➤

STONEHENGE
and AVEBURY

THE WORLD HERITAGE SITE

RODNEY LEGG

HALSGROVE

First published in Great Britain in 2004

Disclaimer
While the author has walked all the routes described in the book,
no responsibility can be accepted for any omissions or errors or for
any future changes that may occur in the details given.

British Library Cataloguing-in-Publication Data
A CIP record for this title is available from the British Library

ISBN 1 84114 360 X

HALSGROVE
Halsgrove House
Lower Moor Way
Tiverton, Devon EX16 6SS
Tel: 01884 243242
Fax: 01884 243325
email: sales@halsgrove.com
website: www.halsgrove.com

Printed and bound by D'Auria Industrie Grafiche Spa, Italy

CONTENTS

USE AS A GAZETTEER

This volume is designed to be used as a gazetteer. Entries have been divided between the Avebury (Part One) and Stonehenge (Part Two) sectors of the World Heritage Site. Each section is treated alphabetically. Photographs are by the author, or from his collection, with additional shots having been taken for him by Stewart Canham, Colin Graham and Tony Pritchard.

Titles of books, where quoted, are given in the text, with other quotations having been taken from lecture notes or contemporary newspaper reports. The best displays of archaeological finds are in Avebury Museum, the British Museum in London, and the Wiltshire county collections in Devizes Museum and Salisbury Museum.

Access details and six-figure Ordnance Survey map references are given at the start of each listing. Current best maps for the purpose are Explorer 157 (Marlborough and Savernake Forest) and Explorer 130 (Salisbury and Stonehenge).

DEDICATION

To Theresa Howe, Grace Parker and Jackie Rodger across the hills in Wincanton.

'The Stones remain; their stillness can outlast
The skies of history hurrying overhead.'
From 'The Heart's Journey', by Siegfried Sassoon

INTRODUCTION

England's premier prehistoric monuments, both in Wiltshire, come as a joint package. In 1986, Stonehenge and Avebury and their associated archaeological sites won the ultimate accolade of recognition under the World Heritage Convention. They were 'inscribed' in the official roll, as a single World Heritage Site, under the auspices of the United Nations Educational, Scientific and Cultural Organisation. Core areas of both clusters of monuments are in the dual care of English Heritage and the National Trust. Each has begun to benefit from long-term projects to restore its ancient settings.

Together, with the National Trust being in partnership with its tenant farmers and supported by the Department of the Environment, Food and Rural Affairs, our heritage guardians have embarked upon one of the biggest landscape

World Heritage Site sign on the road into Avebury from Devizes.

restoration projects in the country. It is putting into effect the greenest of visions, to recreate an expanse of open grassland as a backdrop to the grey stones of Stonehenge, across hundreds of acres of the central core of the southern part of the World Heritage Site. During the twentieth century – despite decades of Trust ownership of this surrounding land – the setting to Stonehenge became increasingly arable, as did most of the Wiltshire chalklands south of the artillery ranges on Salisbury Plain.

These great grain fields have their own character, becoming the 'Fields of Gold' as celebrated in song by Sting, who lives in the neighbouring parish. Barley and wheat are cash cereal crops. The other visual intrusion through this world-class countryside has been traffic, forking in a pincer movement along the A344 and A303 highways, with the A360 forming the third side of a triangle. Towards the turn of the millennium, the cherished view of the stones from car windows became increasingly intimate, as vehicle movements slowed towards gridlock. Sir Jocelyn Stevens, the flamboyant chairman of English Heritage from 1992, galvanised governmental and environmental agencies into a twin-track approach.

Sir Jocelyn Stevens, as chairman of English Heritage, leading the debate on the future of Stonehenge.

Traffic and the stones as seen from Stonehenge Bottom.

The need for a linking section of dual carriageway along the A303 trunk road to the south of the stones has brought about an ambitious scheme for a tunnel as the only solution that will avoid even greater impact on the archaeological landscape. Hopefully we will be provided with the longest feasible option rather than a shorter alternative that leaves a motorway severing the ceremonial avenue approach and spoils the view from Stonehenge to its skyline clusters of burial mounds. With the cars and lorries beneath the ground – not actually under the stones, as some have reported, but 200 metres to the south – the National Trust's reinstatement of grass and grazing can start to provide a worthy setting for the monument:

Grassland restoration is the best way of restoring the sanctity, dignity and integrity of this historic landscape, while balancing the needs of archaeology, farming, nature conservation and visitors.

The latter will be provided with a subliminal Visitor Centre, largely sunk into the ground, accessible from Countess roundabout and screened by trees in the meadows between Countess Road and the River Avon to the east. Potentially award-winning, the imaginative design is the brainchild of Australian architect Peter Clegg, working with Fielden Clegg Associates. From the Countess site, for the benefit of those who choose not to walk a couple of miles, a park and ride shuttle service will be provided. Merging this into the new green landscape is going to be another challenge.

The project is being carried out in partnership with the Trust's tenant farmers, Fiona and Robert Turner, and is being supported by the Countryside Agency's stewardship scheme. Low-density grazing, by sheep and cattle, will be combined with seasonal hay production. The aim is to restore a herb-rich flora. Downland species, which have retreated to the mounds of unploughed barrows and byway verges, include bird's foot trefoil, devil's bit scabious, early gentian, self-heal and wild thyme. These species support butterflies such as the marsh fritillary and provide cover for ground-nesting birds including the skylark and lapwing.

In drawing up the boundaries of the World Heritage Site in 1986, the Unesco arbiters adopted a proposal by archaeologist Paul Ashbee, writing in 1960, that 'Stonehenge and its Avenue, the Cursus, Woodhenge, and Durrington Walls' – plus their surrounding barrow cemeteries – 'should be considered together as a single entity, as should Avebury, the Avenue and Sanctuary, plus Silbury Hill.'

Australian architect Peter Clegg (foreground) and colleague unveiling their design for the new Stonehenge Visitor Centre at Amesbury.

He also made the point that cultural and political power appear to have shifted from one to the other, from Avebury to Stonehenge, both figuratively and physically as sarsen stones of a size suitable for the latter 'can only be found around Avebury'. The key to both lies in Ashbee's 'priest-kings' of the Marlborough Downs and Salisbury Plain.

Avebury and Stonehenge – including Durrington Walls – represent the twin peaks of the British Neolithic period and its Wessex Culture successor. Other contemporary centres, also with some big burial mounds of vassals or princes, were based around similar large henge monuments at Marden, near Pewsey, and at Knowlton and Dorchester in Dorset. These points of purpose and power became the focus of a network of tracks, interlinking ancient ridgeways and distorting the evolving road system in their direction, much as the abbeys did in the Middle Ages. The presence and therefore the problem of the roads goes back to ancient times.

'Each generation receives the Stonehenge it deserves,' J.B. Priestley used to say. In my grandfather's time it was the focal point of Britain's first military

Mrs Gladys Legg and author Rodney Legg, at Stonehenge in 1957.

aerodrome. For my father's contemporaries it was a case of using the cause of restoring the stones as an excuse to dig where they liked. In my time, at age ten in 1957, it was there to be touched and sat upon for the obligatory photograph.

Now issues of crowd control and the imperative of removing the roads from the stones drive the agenda and have been part of my life since joining the ruling council of the National Trust in 1990. Outlining the relationship on the ground with English Heritage, National Trust land agent Julian Prideaux reminded us that we possessed 2,000 acres of the surrounding landscape, including the car park, whereas the Government – through English Heritage – only owned a tiny triangle around stones. I took the opportunity for an interruption and a laugh, 'Julian, I think you'll find it's the Government's bit that people come to see!'

I've listened to Stonehenge archaeologists for four decades, since cycling as a teenager from Moordown, Bournemouth, to the Red House Museum in Christchurch for an evening lecture given by Professor Richard Atkinson. Recent additions to the Avebury and Stonehenge library have come to me from Tony Poyntz-Wright in Taunton who has also taken it upon himself to monitor news from the stones as it appears in the media generally and the pages of *British Archaeology* and *Current Archaeology* in particular.

My view is that ancient circles were primarily cosmic calendars to enable precise calculation, through the phases of the moon and turning points of the sun, of dates for ploughing, planting and harvesting and public events and festivities. The lozenge-shaped stones at Avebury represent the sun (female in the Indo-European world) and the thin ones are for the moon (male in those cultures).

As for Stonehenge, I envisage it having been a place of ceremony and assembly, with the open-plan nature of the stones allowing the community to gather around it and look in through the outer trilithons from the surrounding circle. Clustering around them on the skyline, looking in from the afterlife from their mounds of vivid white chalk, were their ever-present ancestors. That is the wider picture I shall try to keep in mind as the detail unfolds.

AVEBURY WORLD HERITAGE SITE

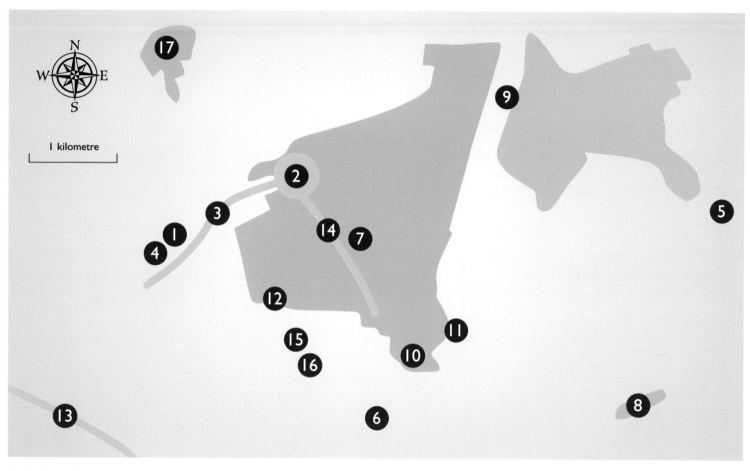

1 Adam & Eve	**7** Falkner's Stone Circle	**13** The Wansdyke
2 Avebury	**8** Lockeridge Dene	**14** West Kennet Avenue
3 Beckhampton Avenue	**9** The Polissoir	**15** West Kennet Henge Monuments
4 Beckhampton Long Barrow	**10** The Sanctuary	**16** West Kennet Long Barrow
5 Devil's Den	**11** Seven Barrows	**17** Windmill Hill
6 East Kennet Long Barrow	**12** Silbury Hill	

National Trust land

Fyfield Down
National Nature Reseve

PART ONE

AVEBURY AREA

Adam and Eve
(SU 089 693: standing stones, Avebury parish, private ownership)

Adam and Eve, otherwise known as the Long Stones or Devil's Quoits, are in Long Stones Field beside Nash Road. William Stukeley (1687–1765) described the setting as Long Stones Cove, and sketched a third stone that had fallen beside Adam. Stukeley coined the word 'Cove' for such arrangements of stones, in nearby Avebury and at Stanton Drew, Somerset.

Eve (left) *and Adam at Beckhampton.*

The crouched skeleton of a man, accompanied by a Beaker food-vessel, was buried beside Adam in the Bronze Age. His presence was revealed after 30-ton Adam fell on 2 December 1911 and the area around was excavated. The Great Western Railway provided three jacks for the re-erection operation carried out by Captain and Mrs Benjamin Howard Cunnington in May 1912. Adam had been virtually placed on the ground with his base being positioned on a slot dug into the chalk that was only 75 centimetres in depth.

Stukeley shows Adam and Eve and their smaller third stone standing in the middle of the Beckhampton Avenue, of which several stones then survived. Three are depicted on the northern side of Long Stones Cove and one to its south. The drawing is only a rough sketch and the depiction is of boulders roughly the same size as the now-missing smaller stone of the Cove. The ploughed remains of a long barrow lie to the east-south-east, aligned from west-north-west to east-south-east, and are crossed by Nash Road.

Avebury
(SU 103 700: Henge monument and stone circles, Avebury parish, National Trust)

The Wiltshire-born antiquary John Aubrey (1626–97) had his first sight of Avebury in 1649. He was enthralled and proclaimed its virtues, saying Avebury 'did as much excel Stonehenge, as a cathedral does a parish church.' These were his words to Charles II, in 1663, and caused the King and the Duke of York – the future James II – to leave the Queen at Marlborough and divert to Avebury for its first royal visit, while the court was en route from London to Lacock and Bath. Aubrey described the method by which 40-ton stones were being felled and destroyed in fiery pits:

After the stone is well heated, draw a line with cold water and immediately give a knock with a smith's sledge, and it will break like collets [collar bands] *at the glasshouse.*

The great bank and ditch at Avebury, second only in size to Durrington Walls near Stonehenge, is a henge monument 425 metres in overall diameter. The ditch is 350 metres in diameter.

These earthworks date from c.3000BC and the stones from 2700–2300BC. The four entrances all appear to be original and each carries a present-day road. The bank is 6 metres high and the ditch is 4.5 metres deep. Its original depth

Adam (left) *and Eve are also known as the Long Stones.*

Above: *Henge bank cyclist in silhouette from the south-west quarter at Avebury.*

Top left: *Post-mediaeval Avebury, its south-west quarter (left) almost cleared of stones, drawn by S. Prout and engraved by J.C. Smith in 1813, looking northwards through the southern portal stones (centre).*

Bottom left: *Bank and ditch of the Henge monument at Avebury, looking north-eastwards in the south-east quarter of the site.*

was 14 metres with a flat bottom, 4.5 metres wide. Today, after 5,000 years of weathering, the bank and ditch make a seamless join. Originally, however, they were separated by a flat platform that acted as a construction corridor, 4.5 metres wide.

The area covered by the Avebury complex was calculated by the antiquarian Sir Richard Colt Hoare as being just over 28 acres. The ground inside is virtually flat and lies at 160 metres above sea level. Having its ditch inside the mound, it was observed from an early time, this could not have been a place of defence.

Avebury had lost most of its meaning and sanctity by Iron Age and Romano-British times as much of the ground inside the Great Circle, even beside and between the stones, was put under the plough. On the other hand the later Anglo-Saxon inhabitants were uneasy about extending this ambivalence to combining the old and new religions. Unlike at Knowlton, in Dorset, the tenth-century Christian church was built outside the henge monument rather than being placed at its centre.

By the time of the Domesday Book, in 1086, Avebury was 'Terra Regis' – the King's land – and its only parcel in arable cultivation, amid the sheep downs, was adjacent to St James' Church. This ground and the nearby Anglo-Saxon building was held by Rainbold the Priest from Pewsey. They retained an unusual 'peculiarly ecclesiastical' status until the time of the Reformation.

Between the reigns of Henry I (1100–1135) and Richard II (1377–99) a 'foreign house' of monks, Benedictines attached to St George of Bocherville, was established at Avebury. The enclosure and its stones passed to New College, Oxford, and then the College of Fotheringay, until 1537 when the first land was released into private ownership. The burial and destruction of the stones had already started. There is no evidence that this was carried out for a religious purpose; it is more likely to have been motivated by the need for clear ground for horticultural and agricultural reasons, with the bonus of some boulders being broken up for building stone, as 'the vile hamlet' expanded eastwards from the High Street and along the Herepath. This begins opposite the 1802-dated Red Lion Inn and is now called Green Street. In the eighteenth century sufficient numbers of the stones remained to indicate what had been lost and William Stukeley calculated that there had originally been 100 stones in the Great Circle.

In 1829, Joseph Hunter recorded that:

Solitary standing stone in the north-east quarter, inside the still impressive bank and ditch at Avebury.

Recumbent stone of the Great Circle, looking east in 1973 along Green Street from the north-east quarter towards the Herepath and the Fyfield Down source of the sarsen stones.

Barber Surgeon's Stone, No. 9, and the Red Lion Inn at Avebury.

... with the last two years, three, if not four of the remaining stones have been broken up, for no other purpose but to form a kind of wall to keep up the earth on the right-hand side of the road to Swindon.

Members of Wiltshire Archaeological Society excavated for a week inside the two inner circles during the autumn of 1865. They found only 'a few bones of animals and some fragments of coarse pottery' which spoilt 'the sepulchral theory which has been so much pressed of late years.' Some of the pottery, however, was Romano-British though, as John Thurnam pointed out, this was only to be expected from 'a place of resort in Roman times'.

The first major excavations at Avebury, 1911–22, were carried out by Harold St George Gray (1872–1963). He concentrated on the Great Ditch. In 1914 he found the skeleton of a smallish adult female who, judging from the degree of silting, had been buried in about 2100BC.

Alexander Keiller (1889–1955), who owned the marmalade company and had already excavated Windmill Hill, bought Avebury Manor and its farm land in the 1920s. Flamboyant and fast-living, remembered as 'a queer cove' with a passion for sports cars, he justified his efforts at Avebury during the Depression as a job creation scheme.

In 1943 when Avebury was acquired by the National Trust, the brothers of the late T.E. Lawrence donated the proceeds of a privately printed first edition of his *Seven Pillars of Wisdom* from Lawrence of Arabia's cottage at Clouds Hill towards the purchase price.

Avebury's Great Circle is about 332 metres in diameter. Some of the biggest stones flank the south and north entrances and stand 5 metres high. As we see the Great Circle today it comprises 27 standing stones, a couple of fallen stones and 16 concrete pillars marking the sites of socket-holes excavated by Keiller between 1934 and 1939. Several of the stones were raised and re-erected, including that known as the Barber Surgeon's Stone on the south-west side, which was named for the tools carried by an individual whose skeleton was found beside it. It is now known, through research by Mike Pitts, that he was a stranger to the parish who died and was pushed into the pit which had been dug to bury stone No. 9 in about 1320. The stone slipped towards the corpse and damaged it. He was in fact a tailor, or such like, rather than a barber surgeon.

The excavator D. Emerson Chapman, taken to task for chopping down trees and demolishing cottages, told his critics in 1938 that there were many trees and cottages in Wiltshire but there was 'only one Avebury in the whole of Europe'. He went on to write that 'years of work will be necessary to excavate and reconstruct the entire site with thoroughness and accuracy.' Alexander Keiller also yearned to complete his work on the other side of the main road. 'But for Hitler,' he lamented, 'we would have finished the job.'

Avebury's stones tend to be either upright pillars or lozenge-shaped diamonds of which the Swindon Stone, on the west side of the main road at the northern edge of the monument, is the perfect specimen. The diamond sort predominate in the Great Circle. Many of them are so consistent in shape that they must have been roughly dressed before being dragged down here from Fyfield Down, on the eastern horizon, via the Herepath.

Inside the Great Circle lay smaller circles and other settings of stones. The Southern Circle and Northern Circle were each about 104 metres in diameter and contained 30 stones. Only nine survive; seven standing and two fallen.

Best preserved segment of the Great Circle, looking east in the south-west quarter, towards the south entrance.

Inside the south-west quarter of the Great Circle, heading towards the trees beside the south entrance.

The huge southern portal stones (top right) *from the restored south-west quarter of Avebury.*

There is flimsy evidence for a far-north Circle as three socket holes, not forming part of the Great Circle, are marked by concrete blocks. They stand beside the northern entrance into the earthwork, crossed by the northern edge of the Great Circle at the Swindon Stone, on the west side of the Swindon Road. No other socket holes were found along their arc – which spoilt a theory that the circle had been demolished in antiquity. If intended as a circle, as the excavator D. Emerson Chapman claimed in 1937, it was never completed. A more likely explanation is that the stones formed an entrance portal, particularly as one that fell and broke in the eighteenth century is said to have been 6.7 metres high.

These three northern stones and those on the west sides of the two interior circles formed a line – north to south – towards a glimpse through the southern entrance to Waden Hill.

The interior arrangements of stones comprise a major setting in the grass to the south of the Nonconformist chapel in the south-east sector and a Cove in the north-east sector, to the north of Green Street. The missing central stone of the Southern Circle was a huge monolith – 6.5 metres high – known as the Obelisk. Its site is now marked by a relatively modest concrete pillar. It was

Central section of the south-west quarter, empty socket holes with concrete markers, looking south-eastwards to trees beside the south entrance.

Swindon Stone (left) *beside the north entrance through Avebury's bank and ditch, looking southwards into the village.*

Looking northwards from the centre of the South Circle.

The north-west quarter, looking southwards to the Red Lion Inn (top left).

North-west quarter of Avebury's Great Circle, westwards to the parish church.

surrounded by a D-shaped arrangement of much smaller stones known as the Z Feature. Six of these survive and the other six have concrete markers. They are off-centre in terms of the surrounding circle.

The Northern Circle, to the east of the Red Lion Inn, has been spoilt by post-mediaeval building. Its surviving features are the two great stones of Cove, which was originally a U-shaped three-stone arrangement. These two remaining stones, each 5 metres high and leaning for as long as anyone could remember, were fenced off in 1997. In April 2002, with the aid of steel jacks provided by Ellis & Company from Shepton Mallet, the National Trust owners and English Heritage guardians set about righting them. What surprised the archaeologists was that both were set far deeper into the ground than anyone could have guessed. Not only were they not unsafe and unlikely ever to fall but they may well have been deliberately set an angle.

The largest of the two stones continues for 10 metres into the ground. This more than doubled its assumed weight, to over 100 tonnes, and thereby put it on a par with the biggest standing stones in the British Isles. Although the contractors and consulting engineers, Mann Williams of Bath, righted the smaller of the stones they left the big one in situ. It still leans but has been

Portal stones (left and centre) *of the Great Circle, northwards across the south-east quarter to the South Circle and Avebury village.*

The Cove, westwards to the adjoining cottage, in 1930.

The Cove (left), eastwards to semi-derelict barns, in 1973.

The Cove, looking south-eastwards to Green Street, in 1975.

The Cove, south-eastwards to Norris' Farm, (left) in 1922.

The stones of the Cove, seen from the west, in 2004.

The great stone at the Cove, estimated to weigh more than 100 tonnes – half of which is underground – looking eastwards to the barn, in 2004.

packed around the base with lime concrete to ensure that it never falls further from the vertical. Neolithic cereal grains, pollen and traces of prehistoric insects were removed for further study by students from the universities of Leicester, Southampton and Wales.

This is our first real clue as to the purpose of Coves at megalithic monuments. It is not possible to half-bury a monstrous stone by accident. It was placed in a great hole with half of it in the earth and the other half in the sky. Its huge bulk linked the two. Coves may well have been the setting for libations and other offerings to the god or gods of earth or its underworld. These were at the opposite spectrum to the sun and the moon as represented by the surrounding circular settings of stones.

Inside the southern entrance, the Ring Stone stood as a single sarsen within the Great Circle, until it was reduced to a stump in the eighteenth century. It was what we would regard as a huge 'lucky stone' and took its name from the natural hole that appears in its mass. To the south, there was a great timber post or totem pole, on the east side of the entrance causeway.

Stone-less here, apparently, but some of the monoliths of Avebury's south-east quarter still lie beneath the grass.

The south-east and north-east segments of the Great Circle are by no means as stone-free as they appear. A geophysical survey, carried out in 2003, revealed that at least 15 of them – about a third of the missing number – still lie intact under the grass, where they were buried to free the ground for mediaeval cultivation or to dispose of pagan icons.

Beckhampton Avenue
(SU 092 695: Sites of standing stones, Avebury parish, private ownership)

The course of the Beckhampton Avenue was recorded by William Stukeley who shows it in 1723 as the western counterpart of the Kennet Avenue. It ran westwards from two stones opposite the churchyard in the High Street and skirted the south side of Bray Street. It then bent south-westwards to pass either side of Adam and Eve – which survive – continued between the Beckhampton Long Barrow and what is now the roundabout at the crossroads of the A4 and A4361.

The end point was in the big open field towards the surviving stretch of Roman road in what has been arable land since the Middle Ages. It is now crossed by horse-gallops.

The Beckhampton Avenue had already suffered a sustained rate of attrition and the final removals were the work of farmer Richard Fowler in the 1740s. As with Avebury, generally, stones were sometimes buried rather than broken-up. Despite this evidence, twentieth-century archaeologists, including aerial reconnaissance pioneer O.G.S. Crawford and Avebury excavator Alexander Keiller, accused Stukeley of having 'imagined' the Beckhampton Avenue in order to support his 'fanciful' conjecture that Avebury had been conceived in the shape of a snake. They had to concede, however, that in making his plan of the West Kennet Avenue, Stukeley was scrupulously accurate. The same can now be said of his depiction of stones in the Beckhampton Avenue.

In 1999 six large mediaeval pits were discovered in the vicinity of Adam and Eve by Andy Payne and Louise Martin in a geophysical survey. An excavation was carried out by Mike Pitts, aided by Mark Gillings, Joshua Pollard and Dave Wheatley.

Three of the holes contained sarsen stones. The holes were 5 metres across, placed between 25 and 30 metres apart, and 17 metres from side to side. These measurements correspond to those of the West Kennet Avenue. Two of the other pits were shallower and packed with charcoal and burnt pieces of stone. The sixth pit was empty. For a time it had contained an intact stone which was later raised and presumably removed for building purposes. The three remaining stones and debris from the other two were reburied at the end of the excavation.

Confirmation of the existence of the Beckhampton Avenue has revived speculation that there was also a Sanctuary-style arrangement of posts or stones in the vicinity of Beckhampton House or to the west of Durran Farm. Just as the Sanctuary faces the eastern sunrise the Beckhampton area has a wide view of the western sunset.

Beckhampton Long Barrow
(SU 087 692: Long barrow, Avebury parish, private ownership)

Large but mutilated and scrub-covered, Beckhampton Long Barrow stands in a paddock, on the north side of the roundabout at the junction of the A4 and A361. It is visible from both main roads opposite Beckhampton House and a byway which passes through the trees on the other side of the field.

Beckhampton Long Barrow, looking scrubby, seen from the south in 2004.

The barrow is 68 metres long by 36 metres wide and 4.5 metres high. Its alignment is south-west to north-east. Excavations have revealed a secondary Beaker burial, inserted in one side of the barrow when it was already old, but the primary inhumations were not found. As there are no signs of any sarsen stones protruding from the mound it is presumed to be an earthen type of long barrow which was raised over skeletons that had accumulated in a rectangular timber mortuary chamber towards the eastern end. Three ox skulls were found along the axis of the mound.

It is regarded as contemporary with the pre-megalithic period of the Windmill Hill peoples and dates from between 3500 and 3200BC in the Neolithic period.

Devil's Den

(SU 152 697: Chambered long barrow, Preshute parish – private ownership)

A cromlech-style setting of stones is visble from the bridleway along Clatford Bottom, a kilometre from the A4, northwards from opposite Clatford Farm between the hamlets of Fyfield and Clatford. Its late Neolithic long barrow mound, 70 metres long by 40 metres wide, was sketched by William Stukeley in

Devil's Den burial chamber and its residual mound in a view over Clatford Bottom.

Among the sarsen stones – known as Grey Wethers – in Fyfield Down National Nature Reserve, above the Devil's Den.

The Devil's Den (centre) as seen from its displaced stones in Clatford Bottom.

1723. It was then strewn with other sarsen stones, perhaps from a crescent-shaped forecourt, but these and the mound have since disappeared.

Only the megalithic burial chamber survives, in splendid isolation in an arable field on the valley floor, rather than a more usual skyline situation. These remains were badly restored in 1921 with a concrete buttress supporting the biggest of the four tilting stones. On these a huge capstone is balanced. This is roughly 3 metres square and 1 metre thick. Its top stands 3 metres above the ground. The displaced stones lie to the east on the valley floor.

The location is at 142 metres above sea level. What little that is left of the Devil's Den enables it to be dated to between 3500 and 2500BC. Its significance is in being the closest megalithic monument to the source of the stones. These can be seen to the north-west, only 500 metres away, and this was the route down which the big stones for Stonehenge may have been hauled. Sarsen-strewn Fyfield Down with its ancient quarries extends for 3 kilometres, upwards to the 250 metre contour, in the vicinity of the Polissoir beside the Ridgeway above Avebury.

Tree-covered East Kennet Long Barrow, forming the skyline above the village, is the biggest of its kind in Britain.

East Kennet Long Barrow
(SU 116 669 – Chambered long barrow – East Kennet parish – private ownership)

The largest long barrow in the British Isles, this great tree-covered mound is 105 metres long, 30 metres wide and 7 metres high. It stands on the north-west side of a chalky spur at 190 metres above sea level. The alignment also matches the edge of this ridge, being from north-west to south-east. Here there are the tops of apparently undisturbed sarsen stones, indicating the presence of Neolithic burial chambers similar to those of West Kennet Long Barrow.

Field archaeologist Leslie Grinsell enthused over this immense but unexcavated chambered long barrow as a prize that has to be left for future generations to explore. He made the point in *The Ancient Burial Mounds of England* in 1953:

> *This magnificent example is in its profile perhaps the most typical of all long barrows, gradually rising up and splaying out towards the 'business end', where protruding sarsens proclaim the existence of chambering. It is to be hoped that excavation of this monument may be the privilege of some future age of archaeological enlightenment.*

Falkner's Stone Circle
(SU 109 694: Stone circle, Avebury parish, National Trust)

Standing in the field boundary 400 metres north-east of the south end of the preserved length of the West Kennet Avenue, just one stone marks the site of this small but significant setting. It stands a metre high, beside a gateway, and a second stone is set – or has been reset – in the hedgerow. Any stone in such close proximity to Avebury has to be regarded as important. The circle stands on the Avebury side of the hedge beside the bend in the hedgerow.

Falkner's Stone Circle has been reduced to a single standing stone, with a clear view across to Avebury Down (top right).

Two other fallen stones were still visible until 1840. Excavation has revealed the socket-holes of another seven stones. Some of the displaced sarsen stones had been dumped in the hedge.

The location is on flat ground at 158 metres above sea level with a contemporary Bronze Age round barrow on the rise 100 metres to the south. North-westwards, Falkner's Stone Circle had an open view to the West Kennet

Avenue, and around deeper countryside to the north and north-west, including Monkton Down and the beech clump and barrows on Avebury Down.

Lockeridge Dene

(SU 144 673: Sarsen stones, West Overton parish, National Trust)

Despite the quantities of choice stones removed in antiquity, particularly the larger ones, the raw materials of the megalithic builders can still be seen across large areas of the Marlborough Down. A dozen acres on the north side of the road at the western end of Lockeridge hamlet represent the easiest accessible example of the remains of this skin of exceedingly hard concrete-like sandstone that formerly covered the chalk formation. Holes in the stone were caused by the roots of palm trees. The layer dates from the Eocene epoch of the Tertiary period, 50 million years ago, and was raised from sea level into hills by upheavals caused by the collision of the earth's tectonic plates.

This land was bought for the National Trust in 1908 by public appeal. The stones here, beside thatched cottages in a picturesque valley, are lying in their natural random order rather than in a man-made arrangement.

Sarsen stones in Lockeridge Dene.

Sarsen stones are also known as Grey Wethers – castrated rams – from their resemblance to grazing sheep. Their older name, sarsens, probably derives from the Saracens. The first disciples of Mohammed, after his death in AD632, Saracen became the shorthand for heathen in Christian Europe as Arab conquerors spread westwards from Baghdad, reaching Spain in AD711. The use of the word for these Wiltshire stones would be indicative of the fact that they were still associated with an alien religion.

Sarsen, as with quartz, is so hard that it can only be effectively cut and carved with bits of itself. Both quartz and sarsen are harder than steel. This has its implications in considering the scale of the work that had to be undertaken to turn the best boulders of the Marlborough Downs into the monument we know as Stonehenge.

Remnants of the layer of sarsen stones in the hamlet of Lockeridge where two fields are owned by the National Trust.

The Polissoir
(SU 128 716: Axe-grinding bench, Winterbourne Monkton parish, private ownership)

Unmentioned by the *Victoria County History* and not shown on the Ordnance Survey map, the discovery of the Polissoir can be credited to a letter writer to *Country Life*, following which industrial chemist George Osborn took me to see it. The triangular stone, 2.4 metres long and 90 centimetres wide, lies knee-high in the grass on downland 150 metres east of the Ridgeway, immediately north-west of Fyfield Down National Nature Reserve. It is one of the first accessible stones as you approach from Avebury, 3 kilometres to the south-west down the Herepath which becomes Green Street, and eastwards there are hundreds more.

At the time of our visit, in 1982, George Osborn and I were collaborating on *Exploring Ancient Wiltshire*. Having demonstrated how Neolithic man had used it to sharpen axes and arrows, leaving six deep gashes in the south end of a sarsen stone, he declared that this was 'the finest example of such a stone in Britain' and the equivalent of examples from France. Hence it was given the French name.

The five and a half grooves of the axe-rubbing Polissoir with a coin for scale (10p) and burnisher beside it (left).

I measured the grooves. They are between 45 and 60 centimetres long. We made the following notes:

At the side is a shallow recess or curvette, smooth to touch, which served as a polisher

Sarsen stones on Fyfield Down, east of the Ridgeway and the Polissoir.

The Polissoir, among the sarsen stones closest to Avebury, was used for polishing stone axes.

or burnisher for the facets of the stone axe. This curvette is about 30 centimetres long and 25 millimetres deep. The area beside it has also been polished smooth. Polissoir is merely the French word for polisher.

The Sanctuary
(SU 119 680: Sacred site, Avebury parish, English Heritage)

Concrete markers in the grass show a layout of two concentric stone circles plus six circles of post holes. The removal of the stones, for 'a little dirty profit', was carried out by builder Tom Robinson in 1724. A crouched burial, with a Beaker, was found beside one of the stone holes.

The Sanctuary found its twentieth-century excavators in the wife and husband team who ran Devizes Museum. Maud Pegge married Captain Benjamin Howard Cunnington, the great-grandson of the Wiltshire antiquary, in 1889. They effectively resumed where he had left off, with articles in the *Wiltshire Archaeological Magazine* from 1900 onwards, until Howard's death in 1950 which was followed by Maud's in 1951.

Renewed interest in the Sanctuary resulted from the pioneer flights in search of archaeological crop marks that began in 1924 through a partnership between Osbert Guy Stanhope Crawford (1886–1957), an observer in the Royal Flying Corps during the First World War, and pilot Alexander Keiller who served in the Royal Naval Air Corps.

The original Neolithic arrangement of timber posts at the Sanctuary is shown by concrete markers. They comprise six concentric circles – the outer one 20 metres in diameter – around a big central post. All the concrete markers that represent posts are circular. The conventional belief that the Sanctuary was a building for community assemblies was effectively challenged by Mike Pitts in 2000, when he suggested that the posts of the second phase of the monument were continually moved as part of regular rituals.

This could be explained by the predicting or recording of lunar rising and setting alignments – which vary in position over a cycle of 18.61 years – as these poles would have tallied with the positions of two pairs of posts in the central ring of phase one. The lunar cycle has four extremes – south-east, south-west,

The prehistoric Ridgeway southwards between a round barrow (top left) *and the hedge beside the Sanctuary* (right) *on Overton Hill.*

north-east and north-west. The moving of posts, for whatever reason, hardly seems consistent with visualising the Sanctuary as a thatched rotunda.

Later, in the Wessex Culture period of the Bronze Age, the remains of the timber structure were removed and the site reconstructed with two circles of sarsen stones. Their positions are now shown by rectangular-shaped concrete blocks. The diameter of the outer ring is 40 metres and the inner one is 13 metres across. The crouched skeleton of a youth had been buried beside one of the stones with a beaker placed between his knees. Such burials, as found beside Adam and some of the stones of the West Kennet Avenue may have ceremonial significance. On the other hand it would seem to be a logical honour to bestow on those who died during the prolonged and dangerous progress of stone-raising enterprises.

The oddest finds, recorded in 1930 from the base of several stone and post holes at the Sanctuary, were unusually large quantities of banded snails, particularly *Cepaea nemoralis*. It is not a species of the dry chalklands. The assumption has to be that the creatures were ritually deposited, because the bright and varied colours of their shells are in maze-like spiral patterns, representing living originals for the swirls of prehistoric art.

Seven Barrows
(SU 120 682: Round barrows, West Overton parish, National Trust)

The local name of Seven Barrow Hill, which field archaeologist Leslie Grinsell traced back to an Anglo-Saxon charter from AD956, has been usurped on the Ordnance map by the less descriptive Overton Hill. Now, however, the National Trust has reinstated Seven Barrows as a name, though the visible number is now down to five. They include a pair of bell barrows with a bowl barrow squeezed between them. A section of Roman road also crosses the Trust's field to the north of the present A4.

South of the main road, a big bowl barrow contained a primary burial in a hollowed-out tree trunk. The skeleton was accompanied by a flat bronze dagger, an axe, and a crutch-headed pin. Barrows hereabouts provided source material for Dr Toope of Marlborough, a renowned quack in the first half of the nineteenth century, whose cure-all was based upon pulverised human bones. He was credited by the antiquarian A.C. Smith with having produced 'a noble medicine, that relieved many of my distressed neighbours.'

Bowl barrow at Seven Barrows, south of the A4.

Bowl barrows at Seven Barrows, north of the A4, with a National Trust grazing team.

The great landmark of Avebury's countryside, Silbury Hill, seen from a farm track across the River Kennet to the south-west.

Silbury Hill, from the main road to the east, showing the ledge (centre, top) *that encircles the conical summit.*

Silbury Hill
(SU 100 686: Artificial hill, Avebury parish, English Heritage and National Trust)

The largest artificial hill in Europe covers 5.5 acres and has a diameter of 167 metres. Conical in shape, with a distinctive flat top 30 metres in diameter, it rises 40 metres high. The angle of the slope is 30 degrees. There is a circular ledge near the top, appearing as a terrace, 4 metres down from summit. The highest point of Silbury Hill stands at 188 metres above sea level.

Around the bottom of the mound, its huge ditch turns into a moat in wet weather, and sometimes becomes such a respectable expanse of water that it is graced by swans. Although it is now largely silted it was originally up to 6.4 metres deep towards the base of the mound and spread out into a great bay on the north-west side. Local folk memory holds that there used to be a circle of stones beyond the ditch.

Silbury starts off from a relatively low point in the landscape. There was a natural spur of downland that projected northwards and this forms the bottom

Swans grazing beside the moat-like ditch west of Silbury Hill.

quarter of the mound. Its base line is on the same contour as Swallowhead Springs, 500 metres to the south, on the intermittent upper reaches of the River Kennet. Had Silbury Hill been built on Waden Hill, which rises naturally to a rounded 191 metres to the north-east, its bulk would look even more enormous. In the process, however, it would have lost the silhouettes of its complex sight-line relationships with other Avebury-related monuments. Often it is only Silbury's cap – above the notches of the terrace – that peeks above the horizon.

The Roman road from Bath to Mildenhall makes an uncharacteristic kink, about 180 metres west of Silbury Hill, to head south-eastwards and avoid the obstacle which had been used as a sighting point by the highway engineers. Sir Richard Colt Hoare suggested they had 'taken Silbury Hill for its bearing' and Professor John Tyndall agreed in 1866 that it was a 'splendid landmark'. Revd A.C. Smith, who frequently passed Silbury on his way from Yatesbury to Marlborough, traced its line close to the monument, both in winter as 'the snow which is melted from the surrounding fields clings somewhat longer to the old road' and summer when 'the crops of corn [are] ripening somewhat earlier on the track of the Roman road.'

In Anglo-Saxon times, through to at least 1281, Silbury was known as Seleburgh. 'Sael' was the Norse harvest festival and 'burgh' or 'bury' was a man-made or fortified hill. The root name is also close to Sul, a Celtic male deity, whose name was adopted at Bath for the Roman hot-water temple of Sulis Minerva at Aquæ Sulis.

Silbury Hill received its first royal visit on the day of the diversion to Avebury in 1663. Before heading off to rejoin the Queen, to proceed to dinner at Lacock, Charles II and the Duke of York 'climbed to the top of it'. They were accompanied by two antiquaries, John Aubrey and Dr Walter Charleton (1619–1707), the latter in his professional capacity as royal physician.

William Stukeley drew iron horse-trappings which accompanied a Viking skeleton, inserted close to the top, which were disturbed when a Mr Holford attempted turning Silbury into a tree-clump in 1722. Drawn by Stukeley, it appears with his original manuscript notes, inserted into a copy of *Abury, a Temple of the British Druids*, which he published in 1743.

It is an attractive notion that this was the burial place of the early Bronze Age chief who built the Avebury stone circles. On the other hand, excavation tunnels have failed to reveal any such origin, although this does not preclude the possibility of the mound having been built as a cenotaph for just such a personage who died elsewhere in a situation which prevented recovery of the body. The first shaft into the mound, vertically from the top, was dug by Cornish engineers in 1776.

Edward T. Stevens, an antiquary who wrote to the *Gentleman's Magazine* in 1829, saw Silbury as 'a huge lingam' – the Hindu phallus, as a symbol of Shiva – being 'to the rest of the temple' at Avebury 'what these sculptured stones themselves were to the figures carved upon their surface.' It shows how the empire was bringing fresh ideas to British pre-history.

Dean John Merewether (1797–1850), who married Mary Ann Baker from Wylye, Wiltshire, included Silbury Hill in his barrow-opening campaign which rampaged across the Marlborough Downs in the summer of 1849. From 18 July to 14 August 1849 that year he dug into between 20 and 30 of the largest mounds. At Silbury, acting under the auspices of the Archaeological Institution, he tunnelled into the centre of the hill from the southern ditch. The resulting report is patchy, although Merewether had a reasonable excuse as this proved to be his last winter. He died in Madeley Vicarage, Herefordshire, on 4 April

The Roman road from Bath, heading for Silbury Hill.

1850. *Diary of a Dean* was published posthumously in 1851 and is an account of what was summarised as the 'Examination of Silbury Hill and of various Barrows and other Earthworks on the Downs of North Wilts.'

Merewether's tunnel, but precious little else, was rediscovered by Professor Richard Atkinson in the excavation of the hill for the cameras in an exciting but uneventful investigation commissioned by BBC Television between 1967 and 1970. Atkinson pushed a slightly larger tunnel into the centre of the hill, also from the south, but from a higher level. He then joined and followed Merewether's route to a point beyond the centre of the hill. Once more it was a case of making news by finding nothing.

What it lacked in treasures was compensated for in terms of knowledge, in particular by establishing its three stages of contraction. There was no king buried in a golden coffin, as local legend predicted, nor the Bronze Age dating that archaeologists expected. Instead, Silbury was put back into Avebury's principal period – adding to its Neolithic heritage of Windmill Hill and the henge monument, and looking across to Beckhampton Long Barrow, West Kennet Long Barrow, East Kennet Long Barrow and the Sanctuary.

Silbury dates from somewhere in the period between 2700 and 2500BC. The herb-rich turf of the original downland, on a natural bulge beneath the mound, survives as a distinct layer only partially bleached by the passage of time. Silbury was erected in three phases, with only short intervals allowing the grass to grow between stages. The basic shape was a three-tier stepped cone which required at least 20 million man-hours of labour. In other words, with a team of 500 people, working a continuous 50-hour a week, the job would have taken 16 years. Allowing for inevitable breaks, if only for the weather and winter, that must have stretched to 20 years. Had they also been required to tend the fields then the work would have spanned a generation. In terms of gross national product, Atkinson made his comparison with the American space mission of 1969, to put man on the moon.

Silbury's structural perfection, from a construction viewpoint, derives from its core of carefully placed chalk blocks and the choice of an outer 30 degree slope. Beloved by modern highway engineers, this ubiquitous angle has been adopted across the world, for cuttings and embankments.

The hill used to feature in the local rites of spring. It was the customary venue for the 'young from the villages around to climb and make merry with ale and cakes.' Palm Sunday was the traditional date for the annual festivities. Silbury Hill has the distinction of having been the second site in Wiltshire – after Old Sarum at Salisbury – to be scheduled under the Ancient Monuments Preservation Act of 1882, by Lieutenant General Augustus Pitt-Rivers from Tollard Royal on his appointment as the first Inspector of Ancient Monuments.

The Wansdyke
(SU 018 672 to 175 666: Linear defences, several parishes, most lengths being beside rights of way)

In April 1809, William Cunnington (1754–1810) travelled from Heytesbury to Lacock for a 'change of air and exercise'. He asked his servant and carriage-driver, John Parker, to go off and investigate the point at which the Wansdyke converges with the Roman road on Morgan's Hill, above Baltic Farm, north-west of Shepherds' Shore. The findings, although correct, contradicted current theories of Wansdyke being a pre-Roman earthwork:

The bank of the Wansdyke, facing towards Avebury, from Shepherds' Shore.

Wansdyke, north-westwards from Shepherds' Shore, above Baltic Farm.

North-facing ditch of the Wansdyke still proving an effective obstacle, looking westwards to Morgan's Hill (top).

Ditch (centre) *and bank of the Wansdyke* (right) *climbing Roughridge Hill, south-east of Avebury.*

I desired him to make some sections at the junction of the Wansdyke with the Roman road; in consequence he has completely ascertained that the Wansdyke is a more recent work. By digging he found that whoever made the Wansdyke cut through the Roman road, for in turning the vallum [ditch] of the former, he came to the original turf covering the curved Roman road.

The defences can be followed along the Wansdyke Path, for 25 kilometres, across the hills south of Avebury. It weaves from Morgan's Hill to Savernake Forest. The palisaded bank and its north-facing ditch date from the collapse of Roman Britain. Such fortifications, including the shorter but stronger Bokerley Ditch across Cranborne Chase, defended the extensive Romano-British settlements of Wiltshire and Dorset from anarchy that threatened from the north.

In this the north-south divide worked at least as well as Hadrian's Wall and the Antonine Wall. The Romanised Britons seem to have been successful in protecting their culture and lifestyle, as no pagan Anglo-Saxon burials have been found to the south of the Wansdyke. Its highest section runs across Tan Hill, called St Anne's Hill in the Middle Ages, which was once the site of a major sheep fair. From the barrow-topped summit, at 271 metres, a significant view ranges from the Black Mountains to Salisbury Cathedral. It is a place where the story of Stonehenge, involving the mass-movement of massive stones from Wales in the west and Marlborough to the north, begins to feel exhaustingly three dimensional.

West Kennet Avenue

(SU 106 695: Ceremonial way, Avebury parish, National Trust)

Evidence of foot traffic towards Avebury along the course of the West Kennet Avenue can sometimes be seen on the ground between its stones. Snow falling on the evening of 28 January 2004 settled on the grass of the actual avenue but failed to do so on the adjacent turf north and south of the double rows of stones. Something must have compacted the ground between the stones to render it harder, and therefore cooler, than that with visually identical grass on either side. Photographs prove that the correlation is a perfect fit.

William Stukeley, in 1723, sketched and mapped 82 visible stones, and plotted the position of a further two that had been buried. A quarter of them, 21 in total, were still standing. Now, however, only 21 are still in existence, of which

Central section of the West Kennet Avenue, gradually converging with the road, looking north-westwards with stone lying on the hard ground between the stones.

Compacted ground of the ceremonial way of the West Kennet Avenue, looking towards Avebury, in the snow of February 2004.

in 1928 only four were still standing and nine partly visible. All precisely corresponded to Stukeley's plan, which archaeologists O.G.S. Crawford and Alexander Keiller found to be 'a priceless document'. They date from between 2300 and 2100BC.

Roadside stones of the West Kennet Avenue, from the south-east, above West Kennet hamlet.

The preserved pairs of stones are 15 metres apart, transversely – from side to side – and 24.4 metres apart longitudinally. Thin pillar-shaped stones – taken by excavators Alexander Keiller and D. Emerson Chapman to represent the male – generally face diamond shaped stones – which they took to be female. That sounds perfectly reasonable but the different shapes might just as easily have represented the moon and the sun. One shrinks into a thin crescent and the other stars like a diamond. Across Indo-European cultures, from Babylon to the Baltic, the moon was regarded as male and the sun as female.

The regular pattern of the stones indicates that originally there were about 100 pairs covering the two kilometres between Avebury and the former south-eastern end of the Avenue on the north-west side of the Sanctuary stone circle on Overton Hill.

Above left: *West side of the West Kennet Avenue, looking towards Avebury.*

Above middle: *East side of the West Kennet Avenue, uphill towards Avebury.*

Above right: *Contrasting shapes of facing stones in the West Kennet Avenue, which probably represent the moon* (male, left) *and sun* (female, right).

Two of the stones have faintly scratched signs of cup-and-ring marks which are so typical of the early Bronze Age in northern parts. Other examples of 'decoration' are often claimed but these are invariably freaks of photography which when seen in the round turn out to be either natural, the result of weathering or fossil root systems. Stones numbered 18 and 25 had contemporary crouched burials accompanied with Beakers. Two other such burials were also found in the vicinity.

The Avenue heads south-eastwards from that entrance to Avebury and maintains that general direction apart from a kink which may have been necessary to avoid an adverse slope or an earlier Neolithic settlement which was found there. The cartographically clumsy way in which stones converge with the present road seems to indicate a realignment to give a gentler approach into the monument. Though comprising only two parallel rows of stones, the West Kennet Avenue is the closest British equivalent to the multiple megalithic rows of Carnac, in Brittany.

The National Trust completed its acquisition of the Avenue with the purchase of 600 acres around West Kennet Farm between 1988 and 1995. The Trust's appeal leaflet made much of 'the Magic of Avebury' and contained this pledge to remove the southern section of the Avenue from arable farming:

With its complete course in its possession, the Trust now plans a geophysical survey of the Avenue's final mile and this will give us the opportunity to consider reinstating such stones as survive under the plough and to record the sites of those that have gone. Ultimately it will bring the whole course under grazing and provide a one and a half mile ceremonial route from Avebury to the Sanctuary.

West Kennet Henge Monuments
(SU 109 683: Henge-type earthworks, Avebury parish, Private ownership)

Visible only from the air, these relics lie near Swallowhead Springs, between West Kennet Long Barrow and Silbury Hill. One is sub-circular, 240 by 220 metres in diameter, and the other ellipsoid in outline, 340 by 200 metres. Both were palisaded, with an estimated 15,000 running metres of oak trunks, which must have given rise to substantial forest clearance and considerable transport difficulties as neither the valley bottom nor surrounding hills had much prehistoric woodland.

The elliptical western earthwork was discovered in 1987 and further air photography revealed the other circle in the dry summer of 1990. Sample excavations by Dr Alasdair Whittle of University College, Cardiff, revealed post holes about 2 metres deep, which had a lining of charcoal indicating the structure had been put to the torch. These holes were in the back-fill of an earlier trench, indicating the site had a complicated history, with sherds of grooved-ware pottery dating from about 2300BC, similar to that found at Durrington Wa56lls, being discovered. The spread of potsherds indicated that the circular enclosure pre-dated the larger elliptical one.

Joints of meat had been buried, as offerings, around the posts. Inside the circular henge monument there was evidence of other features, such as a smaller circle 40 metres in diameter, and two radial ditches led from the main palisade towards the central area.

There were also features outside the elliptical circle, including a palisade that extended south-eastwards, to another small circle.

Enormous portal stones front the east end of West Kennet Long Barrow.

Stepping sideways to enter West Kennet Long Barrow.

West Kennet Long Barrow
(SU 104 677: Chambered long barrow, Avebury parish, English Heritage)

This has been claimed as the largest long barrow in England and Wales. In fact it is the second largest, after its near neighbour East Kennet Long Barrow, which is slightly larger in terms of area, but much bigger in cubic capacity. What makes West Kennet Long Barrow spectacular is that the wedge-shaped mound culminates in an accessible burial chamber and a great line of blocking stones. The largest, the huge central stone, is 3.6 metres high. Grooves on these stones, as at the Polissoir beside the Ridgeway, were caused by the sharpening and polishing of Neolithic stone axes.

Aligned from west to east along a low ridge, West Kennet Long Barrow is 100 metres long by 21 metres wide and rises to 2.5 metres high, around the burial chambers at the eastern end. Side ditches, flanking the long sides of the mound, were 3 metres deep. They survive under the ploughed fields on either side.

Exploring the burial chambers inside West Kennet Long Barrow.

Passage and chambers inside West Kennet Long Barrow, looking westwards and inwards shortly after restoration in the 1950s.

Dr Robert Toope, a friend of John Aubrey from southern Wiltshire, dug into the barrow in the 1680s and it was sketched as a ruin by William Stukeley in 1720. Jumbled and collapsed sarsens protruded at all angles. Despite the dereliction, the original communal burials were still intact when Dean John Merewether opened the mound in the summer of 1849, but he found it difficult to reach them and many skeletons were left in situ.

The eastern entrance, now open to the sky, and the first 5 metres of the passage into the mound were excavated by the craniologist John Thurnam (1810–73) in 1859. He reached six of the burials. The medical superintendent of the County Lunatic Asylum at Devizes, he was looking for material for his studies on *Crania Britannica* and the *Two Principal Forms of Ancient British and Gaulish Skulls*. His ethnic categorisation was based upon skull structure and differentiated between the Neolithic dolichocephalous crania (skulls longer than they are wide) and the brachycephalous crania (short rounded skulls whose widths are at least 80 per cent of their lengths) of Bronze Age peoples. It was pioneering work in analytical anthropology.

Stuart Piggott and Richard Atkinson excavated the remaining four chambers, which contained a total of 20 jumbled and disarticulated burials, in 1955. These were of all ages, from a foetus upwards, and there was only one complete skeleton. The other bones had been tidied into heaps in pre-history. Bone diseases were ubiquitous. All of those who lived to any age suffered from arthritis. Spina bifida was also a common ailment. Piggott and Atkinson came to the conclusion from associated pottery and bone and flint objects and tools that the mound had remained in use for a millennium, from 3500 to 2500BC. Bones of the ancestors seem to have been brought out for ceremonies on high days and holidays.

The total number of burials found during three centuries of archaeology, is estimated to have reached about 50 before the portal stones were closed for the last time. The twentieth-century restoration of the mound has left the chambers, which are partly corbelled, accessible to visitors along an under-ground passage 2.5 metres high and 12 metres long. As well as the end chamber there are two pairs of side chambers. Glass bricks provide light at the end of the tunnel. Ignoring this modern refinement, Colin Renfrew, now Lord Renfrew, sees West Kennet Long Barrow as the archetypal 'realisation in stone of the wooden mortuary chamber of the earthen long barrow.'

Windmill Hill
(SU 086 714: Causewayed enclosure, Avebury and
Winterbourne Monkton parishes, National Trust)

The Neolithic causewayed enclosure on Windmill Hill, north of Avebury, comprises three irregular but approximately concentric ditches and banks which enclose 20 acres of chalk downland. The outer circle is the biggest and deepest, averaging 2.75 metres in depth, although the inner ditch is now particularly conspicuous as it was left open after being excavated by Alexander Keiller from 1924 to 1929. He also investigated the northern parts of the other ditches.

These are interrupted by gaps – hence the original term 'causeway camp' for such earthworks – and each section of ditch seems to have been constructed by its own team of gangers. Around the banks there was probably fencing or blackthorn and hawthorn hedging. The gaps made for easy access into the stockade and were probably sealed by hurdles.

Windmill Hill causewayed enclosure with sections of ditch (right) *outside the bank.*

The body of a dwarf was found in the outer circle and dated from around the time of its construction. He may have been selected or sacrificed as a foundation burial during the building of the stockades. There was, however, an earlier stage of Neolithic cultivation and occupation across the hilltop. A later excavation, in 1957, revealed the post holes of a building or ceremonial structure beneath the outer bank on its eastern side.

Occupation debris from the time of the enclosures included poleaxed ox skulls. The biggest were from the giant wild auroch, an ancestor of modern domestic cattle, made extinct by prehistoric man, and I have an almost contemporary statuette of this long-horned creature in orange Bronze Age ceramic. Midden, or dunghill, material dates from between 4000 and 2500BC. Exhibits in Avebury Museum include antler combs and saucer-shaped rubbing stones which were used for de-husking grain. Theirs was mixed agriculture of arable farming augmented by animal husbandry. The inhabitants used the enclosures as a cattle pound. Multiple enclosures were needed for breeding, herding and protecting their goats, pigs and sheep. Game, brought back from hunting trips with dogs and arrows, also featured in the menu. Inhabitants went out into the countryside to forage on nature's autumn harvest of blackberries, crab-apples and hazelnuts. Camp fires were commonplace, especially in the outer ditch, which seems to have been used as a shelter by herdsmen and was the interface between the stockades and the great open spaces of the wider world.

There is also a cluster of later Bronze Age burial mounds. Nothing is known of the contents of Picket Barrow, a bell barrow, which is 25 metres in diameter and 2.75 metres high. The two bowl barrows to the east are 18 metres in diameter and 2 metres high. The eastern mound covered an inhumation that was accompanied by a grape cup – named for its shape, like a small bunch of grapes – and a perforated battle-axe of volcanic Welsh rock, from Cwm Mawr, Montgomeryshire. Such choice pieces of stone were widely traded and travelled far from their source. Further east lie a pair of saucer barrows, the western one being 25 metres in diameter, and the other 26 metres.

STONEHENGE WORLD HERITAGE SITE

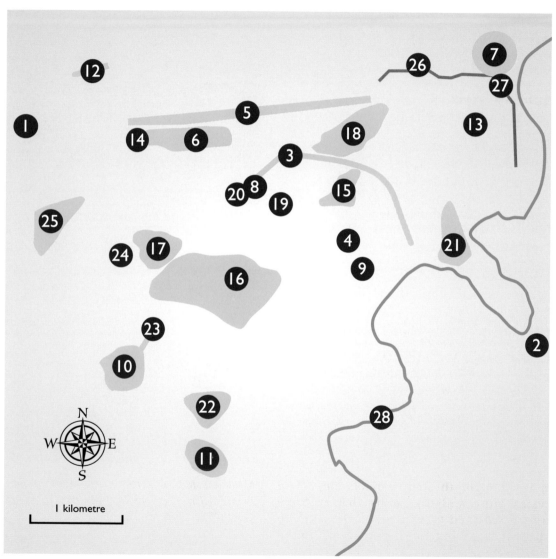

1 Airman's Cross
2 Amesbury Archer
3 The Avenue
4 Coneybury Hill
5 The Cursus
6 Cursus Barrows
7 Durrington Walls
8 Heel Stone
9 King Barrow
10 Lake Barrows
11 Lake Down Barrows
12 Lesser Cursus
13 Military Railway
14 Monarch of the Plain
15 New King Barrows
16 Normanton Down Barrows
17 Normanton Gorse Barrows
18 Old King Barrows
19 Road Network
20 The Stones
21 Vespasian's Camp
22 Wilsford Barrows
23 Wilsford Down Earthworks
24 Wilsford Shaft
25 Winterbourne Stoke Barrows
26 Wood Road
27 Woodhenge
28 River Avon

1 kilometre

PART TWO
STONEHENGE AREA

Airman's Cross
(SU 098 429: Aviation relic, Winterbourne Stoke parish, highway verge)

Though shown as Airman's Corner on the Ordnance Survey map, Airman's Cross as it more accurately appears on detailed aviation charts is a stone memorial cross beside the crossroads at the north-western corner of the World Heritage Site. It stands on a triangle of grass on the junction of the A360 with the A344. Predating both the Royal Flying Corps and Royal Air Force, the Airman's Cross is in fact named for Army airmen, plural, as its inscription records:

To the memory of Captain Eustace Broke Loraine, Grenadier Guards, and Staff Sergeant Richard Hubert Victor Wilson, Royal Engineers, who whilst flying on duty, met with a fatal accident near this spot on July 5th, 1912. Erected by their comrades.

During the First World War, a large aerodrome was constructed south-west of Stonehenge, towards Longbarrow Crossroads, with its main buildings standing either side of the A303 to the north of Normanton Gorse. Lines of huts, laid out on a grid pattern from south-east to north-west, were dominated by a huge hangar on the north side of the main road. Some 40 years later, a wartime veteran of the Royal Flying Corps told archaeologist Richard Atkinson that it had been 'seriously suggested' that Stonehenge should be removed, as a hazard to flight. In the event it was Stonehenge Aerodrome that was decommissioned after the conflict.

This land, covering 1,438 acres, was bought through a public appeal in 1927–28 and vested in the National Trust, with the result that all these buildings were cleared and the ground returned to agriculture. It was deep ploughed, causing considerable damage to all but the visible above-ground archaeology, and considerable quantities of brick, concrete and other twentieth-century debris can be seen across much of the area.

Memorial stone at Airman's Cross to the victims of Britain's first fatal military powered flight on 5 July 1912.

Another memorial to a pilot – Major Alexander William Hewetson of the Royal Field Artillery who was killed in a flying accident on 17 July 1913 – has a view of the Cursus Barrows (background).

Amesbury Archer
(SU 165 415: Burial site, Amesbury parish, rescue excavation)

The grave of the Amesbury Archer was uncovered during an excavation in suburban Amesbury, between the appropriately named Stonehenge School and Boscombe Down, on a site which had already revealed a small Romano-British cemetery and a Bronze Age inhumation. These were then eclipsed by an internationally important discovery. Though just beyond the World Heritage Site, on the east side of the River Avon, its Stonehenge credentials were impeccable. This turned into the most well-endowed early Bronze Age burial ever found in Britain.

The big find took place on a Friday afternoon, ahead of a bank holiday weekend, and digging continued into the night of 2 May 2002. The first indication of its importance was the finding of a gold hair-tress ornament. Below it, inside a timber mortuary enclosure which had probably been covered by a burial mound, was the skeleton of a man. Aged around 40, he had been buried on his left side, in a flexed position, with his face to the north. The bones showed a lopsided gait, resulting from a lame leg, caused by a wound to the left knee. His teeth provided forensic evidence that had grown up in a colder climate. Oxygen isotope analysis by Paul Budd and Carolyn Chenery indicated that he originated from somewhere between the Alps and the Baltic. Radiocarbon dating placed the burial between 2400 and 2100BC.

Orange fabric Beaker pottery included two vessels decorated with bone-comb decoration in typical Wessex Culture patterns. Two other bowls had the earliest kind of all-over plaited-cord decoration. Other grave goods were those of an archer, including 15 barbed-and-tanged flint arrowheads from a quiver of arrows that were scattered above him. He wore a black sandstone bracer on his left arm to protect it from the whiplash of the bow. There was a second, in red sandstone, beside his knees. A bone pin had probably clasped a leather cloak and there was a ring of Kimmeridge shale that most likely clasped his belt. The warrior's personal weapon was a copper knife which had probably been sheathed. Its metal was of Spanish origin. There was no trace of his bow, which, as a single supple yew rod, could have rotted away without trace.

Accompanying items included two pairs of boar tusks. There were two more copper knives, also of Spanish origin. A cache of flints comprised both mint-

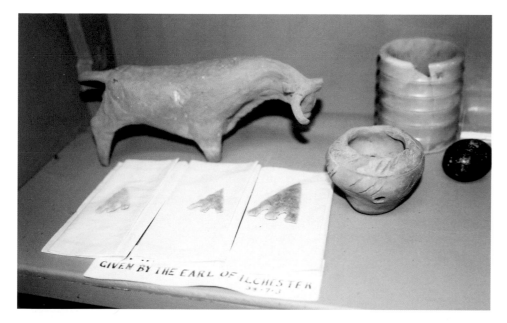

Orange ceramic auroch statuette, of a prehistoric wild cow, with barbed-and-tanged arrowheads and other Wessex Culture finds.

Perforated stone battle-axe and bell-shaped Beakers, which probably contained food or drink for the afterlife, among the commonest Wessex Culture grave goods from barrows around Stonehenge.

condition and used tools with some of the latter having been broken. They
might have formed the archer's personal took kit. They were found with a
small cushion-shaped stone of the type used by metalworkers. Three deer-
antler spatulas may have been used for working flints or intended for carving
into pins. Two earrings were probably of continental origin.

The excavation, by Andrew Fitzpatrick of Wessex Archaeology, had already
located and removed the burial of what is now regarded as the warrior's son.
Aged about 23, he was 5.5 metres away, and had pair of gold earrings or hair-
tresses which seem to have been suspended around his neck from a cord. Once
again there was a forensic sequel. Jackie McKinley found both skeletons had
articulated insteps – a rare condition that does not cause any problems – which
suggested a genetic link.

The number and type of grave goods led Ed Baker of Bournemouth News
agency to dub the main burial as being that of the 'King of Stonehenge'. This
secured national headlines. The title goes far beyond the evidence but the
number of beakers and arrowheads were unprecedented for a single burial
and the metal objects were state-of-the-art for their time. Announcing that
radiocarbon dating confirmed the grave as being from about 2200BC, Andrew
Fitzpatrick described the finds as 'a collection of objects without compare
in Britain, or indeed in western or central Europe.' This nouveau riche
alchemist, whether a pilgrim or settler, may have brought with him metal-
working technology from the Continent.

The location of the burial, close to the River Avon, draws attention to the
waterway's importance as a prehistoric highway, and points to an equal role for
the lowlands which tend to have been overlooked by antiquarians and archaeologists who have always looked to the hills. Durrington Walls and Stonehenge
have ceremonial ways that lead down to and from the river.

The Avenue
(SU 124 423 to 143 414: Ceremonial way, Amesbury parish, partly National Trust)

Linking Stonehenge with the River Avon, 4.5 kilometres away, the Avenue was
built in one operation during the Bronze Age. The section stretching in a straight
line for 550 metres north-eastwards from the stones, shows signs of having originally continued in that direction in the northern end of Stonehenge Bottom. The

Stonehenge (left) *and its Avenue* (centre), *visible as a faint line in the grass, looking south-westwards from the King Barrows ridge.*

route here was designed to approach Stonehenge from the north-east, towards the direction of midwinter sunset, *id est* the south-west. Looking the other way, from the stones, you face the midsummer sunrise.

It was then turned, with a bend, to head eastwards and upwards into the slight dip in the ridge at King Barrows. Here it passed between barrow No. 33 of Old King Barrows, to the north, and No. 32 of New King Barrows to the south.

The straight section in Stonehenge Bottom is 27.5 metres wide, between parallel banks with ditches on the outside, with a height of 0.3 metres between the bottom of the ditch and the top of the bank. The central area, between the banks, is 13 metres wide. Though now restored to grass by the National Trust in the 1980s, most of this part was under the plough until recent years. The line can also be traced uphill towards King Barrows. An apparent left turn, up the valley bottom towards the Cursus, has no connection with the Avenue – as William Stukeley supposed – but represents a much later trackway.

From the ridge at King Barrows, beyond which it has been ploughed not for decades but centuries – and went unrecognised until O.G.S. Crawford studied wartime aerial photographs in 1923 – the Avenue ceases to be visible on the ground. It turns south-eastwards to pass between levelled barrows No. 100 and 131 to the north of the A303 and No. 98 (ploughed flat) and No. 38 (still visible) to the south of the main road. Here there is the suggestion of a slight kink which indicates that these barrows were already in existence. Having crossed Stonehenge Road, west of Vespasian's Camp, the Avenue dropped down to the River Avon. It is not a direct route but does follow the easiest gradients.

Because of its length, there have been numerous small excavations as cables, pipes and roadworks have been cut through its banks and ditches. Several have revealed antler picks and there are numerous bluestone chips in the ditch of the length through Stonehenge Bottom. Radiocarbon dating of antlers and bone date the construction of the Avenue to between 2400 and 2050BC. Mike Pitts propounds the view that it was designed for the approach of funeral cortèges coming from Durrington Walls, via the River Avon, to the newly built Stonehenge.

The Avenue also seems to follow the route that had been used on the final length of the marathon journey that saw the Welsh bluestones brought to the

monument in about 2100BC. It is significant that the Avenue widens to about 33.5 metres before reaching the River Avon in a paddock below West Amesbury House. This unexcavated area may contain a landing stage and storage space originally used for newly arrived stones.

The entire length of the Avenue and land to the north of it continued to be respected through Iron Age and Romano-British times, not being brought into the series of Celtic fields. Understanding its course from a map is easier than trying to see it on the ground. Its use should be visualised from east to west, from the river to the stones, rather than the other way round. Having such an Avenue as the entrance to the stones implies that this was the only dignified and respectful way for the living to approach the monument for assemblies and ceremonies, marriages and other rites of passage that are assumed to have taken place.

For the dead it may also have marked the beginning of their journey into the next world. They came from the direction of sunrise to a funeral in the stones and a barrow burial in the sunset beyond.

Coneybury Hill
(SU 134 416: Henge monument, Amesbury parish, National Trust)

The outline of a Neolithic henge monument, utilised by medieval rabbit warreners, lies on the flat-topped knoll south-east of Stonehenge. Coneybury Hill rises to 115 metres above sea level and is visible from the stones, towards Amesbury, on the skyline. Its earthworks have been levelled by centuries of ploughing, since before 1562 as part of the Middle Field of West Amesbury, and the site is still on arable land.

Aerial photographs have revealed an oval ditch 45 metres in diameter running north-west to south-east and 55 metres from south-west to north-east. The bank was on the outside of the ditch. As with the earthen henge at Stonehenge, Coneybury's single entrance faces north-east, towards Woodhenge. There are a few Bronze Age barrows in the vicinity, all but one also ploughed out, and the alignment of New King Barrows points southwards to Coneybury Hill.

This earthwork may well be one of the 'two round coney-berrys' made or adapted on the instructions of the Earl of Hertford, who owned Amesbury Abbey, in 1605. Rabbits remained a valuable resource – rather than a pest – for more than half a millennium after their introduction by Norman invaders. 'Fourteen couple of conies' were put into the ground by his lordship and 'with their increase did breed and feed there'. Rabbits did as rabbits do, and would be blamed for collapsing parts of Stonehenge and damaging barrows and other earthworks, although their contribution has been no match for that of two-legged vandals and vermin.

The Cursus
(SU 109 429 to 138 433: Ceremonial monument, Amesbury parish, National Trust)

The first of several such long parallel-sided Neolithic enclosures to be discovered on the Wessex chalklands, the Cursus north of Stonehenge was named by William Stukeley for a racecourse. Although consistent with this in appearance there is no evidence for such a use and the juxtaposition of contemporary long barrows implies a sacred purpose. It appears to have been a ceremonial avenue and can be seen from one end to the other, eastwards from a gap in Fargo Plantation which the National Trust cleared of scrub and trees in 1983. The

Bank at the west end of the Cursus with a bowl barrow inside its banks (top left) *and Monarch of the Plain bell barrow in Fargo Plantation* (right-hand side).

Faint lines of the Cursus (centre left and centre right) *heading west towards the barrow in the gap between two sections of Fargo Plantation* (top).

Best preserved length of the Cursus (centre), *north of the Cursus Barrows* (top), *with lesser traces in the foreground* (behind fence).

eastern end is beside a strip of woodland south of Larkhill where the slight traces of a long barrow, aligned from north to south, lie on the eastern side of the trees 40 metres away.

The length of the earthwork, which runs from west to east, is 2,700 metres. At either end it is 100 metres wide but gradually widens to 150 metres in width to the north of the main mounds of the later Cursus Barrows, 650 metres from the west end. To the east of Fargo Plantation, for more than a kilometre, the bank survives visibly and physically, being about 6.5 metres wide and up to 0.4 metres high, flanked by an outer ditch 6 metres wide and 0.3 metres deep. Further east, although almost entirely ploughed out, the line sometimes shows as a colour change in the grass during dry summers or in low-angle midwinter sunlight.

Gaps in the Cursus are almost certainly later breaks rather than original entrances. It dates from between 3150 and 3000BC. No historic internal divisions cross the Cursus apart from at the western end. Here the Amesbury and Winterborne Stoke parish boundary follows the west side of Fargo Plantation and there is also a low bank that crosses the Cursus, obliquely, immediately east of barrow No. 56. Including the ditch, on the west side, the earthwork measures 6 metres across. Its bank runs parallel to the nearby parish boundary.

On the south side its ditch cuts into the bank of the Cursus, indicating it is a later feature, possibly cut as a boundary when the end part was used for Bronze Age burials. A prehistoric walker who continued straight ahead from the Cursus, eastwards across the downs, would have come to a standing stone in 1,000 metres and Woodhenge in 1,400 metres.

The entire length of the Cursus is in National Trust ownership. The main length was acquired in 1927 with the bulge in the Trust's boundary fence which brings in its western end having resulted from the gift of 1.5 acres by J. L. Turner in 1966.

As with the Avenue, the entire length of the Cursus and its nearby barrow cemetery were respected through the Iron Age and Romano-British periods, being exempted from cultivation by Celtic fields.

Cursus Barrows
(SU 118 428: Barrow cemetery, Amesbury parish, National Trust)

Eastwards from the Monarch of the Plain bell barrow, in the south-west corner of Fargo Plantation, the 12 mounds of the Cursus Barrows stretch in a line for a kilometre along the slight ridge between the western end of the Cursus and the north-west side of Stonehenge. Another mound, Amesbury bowl barrow No. 54 lies in Fargo Plantation, towards the Cursus, and bowl barrow No. 56 and levelled bowl barrow Winterbourne Stoke No. 30 actually lie inside the western end of the Cursus.

In No. 30, William Cunnington found a cremation without grave goods, according to Sir Richard Colt Hoare (1758–1838) in 1810. Re-excavation by Mrs P.M. Christie in 1959 revealed a second unaccompanied cremation in a central pit and the crouched skeleton of a child, apparently covered by flints, in the primary silting of the ditch. There were also disturbed fragments of a globular urn as well as later scatters of Iron Age and Romano-British potsherds (broken ceramic material). In a hollow, contemporary with the Cursus rather than the Bronze Age barrow, Mrs Christie found a deposit of pine charcoal and calcimined flints.

Amesbury barrow No. 54 was excavated by Colt Hoare, in 1805, who re-dug an earlier hole. The infill contained several finds, now in Devizes Museum,

The linear Cursus Barrows (centre) *seen from Stonehenge Down, to the south-east.*

including a fine Preselite battleaxe from South Wales, and a short bronze dagger which had been attached to its handle by three rivets. There was also a piece of skull. Elsewhere in the bowl barrow, probably from its primary interments, were fragments of three Beakers, and two sets each of three barbed-and-tanged flint arrowheads. There was also evidence for pre-barrow use of the land with fragments both of earlier Neolithic and Peterborough wares more typical of the valleys towards the Wash.

Southwards, also in Fargo Plantation, are the Monarch of the Plain (see its separate entry) and Amesbury bowl barrow No. 53. The other mounds, as you continue eastwards into open downland, are bowl barrows Nos. 52, 51, 50, 49 and 48. Then come bell barrows No. 48, 47 and 46 (twinned), 45, 44 (actually a pair) and 43.

Bowl barrow No. 51 contained a secondary cremation with beads of amber, faience (decorated and glazed eartheware and porcelain) and stone found by William Stukeley. He also discovered a much later – probably Anglo-Saxon – secondary skeleton. He failed, however, to locate the primary cremation which was left for William Cunnington to find.

Stukeley also opened a pair of twinned bell barrows, with workmen provided by Lord Pembroke of Wilton House, during his Wiltshire explorations of 1723. The antiquarian found 'a layer of flints, humouring the convexity of the barrow' at a metre below the surface. The flints, a foot in thickness, rested on 'a layer of soft mould' also a foot thick, in which Stukeley found an urn containing partially burnt bones and the remains of a long string of blue beads. There were also lozenge-shaped pieces of amber and traces 'of a thin film of pure gold'. The feminine touches led Stukeley to conclude that 'this person was a heroine, for we found the head of her javelin in brass.'

The layout of the barrow cemetery was a little more complicated, as levelled Amesbury barrows No. 114, 158 and 48a are in close proximity, with No. 115 a little further to the south. There were also barrows west of the Monarch of the Plain. Here Winterbourne Stoke barrows No. 29, 28, 82 and 81 were flattened during the building of aircraft hangars and a military railway in 1915.

William Stukeley pointed out the relationship between Stonehenge and its barrow groups, which are generally 'upon elevated ground, and in sight of the temple of Stonehenge.' Beyond, the pattern continues: 'Upon every range of hills, quite round Stonehenge, are successive groups of barrows, for some miles.'

Durrington Walls
(SU 150 437: Henge monument, Durrington parish, National Trust)

This is a huge sacred site with a henge-type bank and ditch in the north-east corner of the World Heritage Site. The outer bank, although largely spread and filled as a result of arable farming during the Middle Ages as part of Durrington Field, has left scarped slopes of dense scrub around the west side of the bank and field. These centuries of tillage left 'its form much mutilated' – as Sir Richard Colt Hoare noted in 1810 – but the western bank still rises 5.5 metres above the interior.

This and the lesser traces around the north-east side surround a bowl-shaped valley. The earthworks are almost circular with an overall diameter of between 468 metres and 490 metres. The eastern houses of Larkhill stand on the west side of the outer bank and a bend in the River Avon lies to the east of the monument. Here the lowest point in the valley dropped between settings of post holes into an avenue of about 60 metres leading to the waterside, which appears to have been a contemporary access point about 22 metres wide. Inland, towards Larkhill, the north-west entrance was 29 metres wide.

The bank was 30 metres wide. Inside, separated by a berm (a flat area) ranging in width from 6 metres at the north-east to 42 metres on the south-west side, are the indications of what was – and still is, beneath the ground – 'an immense ditch' as excavator Geoffrey Wainwright (born 1937) has described it. His sections revealed that it was 17.6 metres wide at the top, 5.5 metres deep, and 6.7 metres wide across its flat bottom.

The ditch is partly visible as a grassy lynchet, from west to east along the south side, where it is crossed by the old course of the A345 road, northwards from Woodhenge. This road went through a third opening in the former double earthworks. It is now a cul-de-sac, having been replaced by the present embanked line of Countess Road in 1967. Wainwright's excavations in 1966, ahead of the new road project, cleared its course and revealed two settings with circles of post holes.

Durrington Walls (top), *visible from the present A345, forming the north-east corner of the World Heritage Site.*

The ceremonial approach to Durrington Walls was up this hollow (centre left) *from the River Avon.*

The northern of these circles was 18 metres in diameter and had four much larger internal post holes with pit ramps beside them. It seems to have been constructed in two phases.

The southern circle lay inside the river-facing entrance to the monument and was developed in two stages. The earliest, of four concentric rings between 2.3 and 30 metres in diameter, was superseded by a much more sophisticated arrangement with a density of posts similar to nearby Woodhenge. This later setting comprises six concentric circles from 5.6 metres to 38.5 metres in diameter.

Outside the entrance of the southern circle, burning had taken place on a platform of chalk blocks surrounded by an area of flint gravel, strewn with pottery, flints and animal bones. There was also a midden, in a hollow 12 metres wide, on the north-east edge of the circle.

Large post holes flanked an entrance that faced south-east towards an avenue and the river. Traces of banks and parallel rows of posts or pits, between the earthworks and the river, were confirmed by a magnetometer survey conducted by the University of Sheffield in 2003. Mike Parker-Pearson speculates that this was the funerary and processional route to the River Avon, which remains the visual focus of the monument.

Aerial photographs and geophysical surveys have also revealed numerous other post holes across much of the interior. A double-ditched inner circle, near the middle of the western half, was 35 metres in diameter overall, with the inside circle being 20 metres in diameter.

Domestic debris indicated that Durrington Walls was a settlement as well as a ceremonial monument. Geoffrey Wainwright calculated that the ditch and bank alone had required nearly a million man-hours in construction terms. Given this was the major construction project of its time for a motivated community, one can visualise the efforts of 200 people, working a 50 hour week for two years. It may, however, have had to fit in between the normal demands of the agricultural year, in which case a decade would seem more reasonable.

Finds from the site have included Neolithic grooved-ware and secondary Beaker pottery and bones. Radiocarbon dates for the latter ranged from between 2714 and 2300BC for the earliest Neolithic settlement, to between 2105 and 1887BC for the internal circles. Bronze Age hearths in the ditch dated to between 1790 and 1490BC.

Durrington Walls and its surroundings, including Woodhenge and the ground westwards to a standing stone and across to the Cursus, continued to be respected in Iron Age and Romano-British times. The Celtic field systems stay clear of all these monuments. Most of Durrington Walls, south-westwards from the A345 at the roundabout beside Stonehenge Inn, was bought by the National Trust in 2002. This holding links with the fields of Countess Farm which was acquired in 1999. At the time of writing the Trust's Stonehenge Estate extends for 6 kilometres, to a point 50 metres east of Longbarrow Crossroads on the parish boundary above Winterbourne Stoke.

Heel Stone
(SU 123 422: Standing stone, Amesbury parish, English Heritage)

Sarsen No. 96 at Stonehenge stands inside the Avenue, on the outside of the henge bank around Stonehenge, 60 metres north-east of the stones. An unhewn boulder, more than 2.5 metres thick, it rises to a point 4.5 metres high, with another 1.5 metres set in the ground. The Heel Stone name seems to have been transferred across the monument from Sarsen No. 14, on the south-west

The Heel Stone (top right) *and Stonehenge performing a wartime propaganda purpose before D-Day with Prime Minister Winston Churchill* (right) *sharing Britain's cultural heritage with General George Marshall, Chief of Staff of the United States Army* (centre) *and Richard Gardiner Casey* (left), *Australian Minister to the United States of America.*

side, where the name would fit as it has a foot-shaped depression and matches John Aubrey's description of what he called the Friar's Heel in 1660.

Excavation around it, as far as the road, was carried out by Lieutenant-Colonel William Hawley in 1923. Re-excavation, by Richard Atkinson in 1953, revealed a fragment of late-Neolithic Windmill-Hill-type pottery from a pocket of 'fine earthy filling' which 'could only be accounted for by the decay of the anti-friction stakes which originally lined the side of the stone hole.' These had cushioned the stone and prevented it from embedding in the side of the hole 'when it was hauled upright.' Hawley discovered another hole and disturbances on the west side of the stone, which were dug again by Atkinson in 1958 and shown to have been 'the ramp used in setting up the stone.'

Atkinson had reached the rammed filling – crushed firm by stones – below the Heel Stone in 1953 and found 'a fragment of freshly fractured bluestone' that dated the erection of the stone to the same period as the Stonehenge bluestones. To the east, the outer bank of the Avenue 'overlies the filling of the Heel Stone's ditch'.

The stone made its contribution to contemporary history during the Second World War. To make a point for international consumption about shared

The Heel Stone seen from the west, with a pair of starlings sitting on top and two visitors outside the wire.

The Henge entrance (right) *and the Heel Stone* (centre) *from the west.*

The Heel Stone (left) *and Stonehenge, with visitors for scale, profiled against the snow in their wider looking setting north-westwards to the hills above Netheravon.*

cultural links, Prime Minister Winston Churchill posed beside the Heel Stone with Stonehenge in the background, in the winter of 1943–44. He was accompanied by the Australian Minister to the United States, Richard Gardiner Casey, and General George Marshall, Chief of Staff of the United States Army.

The 'enormous hole' which held the Heel Stone's missing partner, beside the roadside fence, was discovered by Mike Pitts in an excavation during the summer of 1979. It had been filled with compacted chalk rubble. Sarsen flakes confirmed the former existence of the stone. Between them, the pair of massive megaliths had marked the sunrise corridor, of the midsummer solstice.

King Barrow
(SU 135 416: Round barrow, Amesbury parish, National Trust)

Amesbury bowl barrow No. 23, south-east of the ploughed-out henge monument on Coneybury Hill, was excavated by William Stukeley in 1723. He found 'a very large brass weapon of 20 pounds weight, like a pole-axe'. It has since been lost but a big whetstone, said to have come from this burial mound, is in Salisbury Museum.

Stukeley's weapon continues to excite speculation. Pre-eminent field archaeologist Leslie Grinsell suggested in the 1950s that it was a metal-shafted halbert of the type known from eastern Germany. Pendants have been found in several other Wessex Culture graves, representing miniature halberts, and full-sized objects are known from Scottish and Irish burials.

Lake Barrows
(SU 109 402: Barrow cemetery, Wilsford cum Lake parish, private ownership)

This Neolithic long barrow, aligned north-west to south-east, is 42 metres long, 23 metres wide, and 2.5 metres high. It lies in the south-east corner of Lake Wood, east of the byway halfway between Normanton Down and Druids Lodge, on the A360. The wood is on the 110-metre contour along a flatish ridge.

Northwards and eastwards lies a cemetery of Bronze Age burial mounds in relatively random order. It comprises 15 bowl barrows, up to 30 metres in diameter and 3 metres in height, four bell barrows, up to 45 metres in diameter and 3.5 metres high, and two disc barrows of 55 metres diameter.

Known as the Prophet Barrow – because a French missionary preached from it in 1710 – a bowl-shaped mound covered a pit with a cremation in a wooden coffin that was accompanied by a bronze dagger and a slate pendant. One of the bell barrows had been raised over the body of a four-year-old child who was provided with a beaker which probably contained food. The majority of the other mounds had been placed over cremations and contained a variety of grave goods including bronze daggers, knives and awls, bone pins, an incense cup, and beads of amber, faience, shale and bone.

Seven of the ploughed barrows beside Lake Wood were excavated by Professor William Grimes in 1959. Close to the find-spot of the incense cup, on the inner side of the ditch of bowl barrow No. 36f, satellite burials comprised a male and female, the latter with child. Sherds of a Barrel urn from another mound matched fragments found in a rabbit-scrape in 1950 and were found to have contained cremated bones. Another barrow covered a burial pit which had already been dug by William Cunnington as it contained one of his lead excavation plaques, dating from 1804.

Bowl barrow No. 38 covered seven pits, mostly with collared urns and cremation burials, but some only contained ash and charcoal. Two cremations were of adults, and one was of an infant, but other traces of burnt bones were not identifiable.

A barbed and tanged arrowhead and other worked flints were found in bowl barrow No. 39. A biconical urn contained no traces of a cremation. The same applied to an upright collared urn in ring-ditch No. 90.

Lake Down Barrows
(SU 117 393: Barrow cemetery, Wilsford cum Lake parish, private ownership)

The nuclear cemetery of burial mounds on Lake Down, east of Druids Lodge and above Spring Bottom, comprises ten bowl barrows, five pond barrows, one disc barrow and a saucer barrow. Old excavation accounts indicate cremated bodies were subjected to urn burials – one such miniature pot was uncovered in the disc barrow. Apart from this one, the contents of these mounts were otherwise poorly recorded.

Lake Down and its barrows, with only one being clearly visible outside Lake Wood (right), *looking north-eastwards to Normanton Down* (middle distance, left).

Lesser Cursus
(SU 104 435 to 107 435: Ceremonial way, Winterbourne Stoke parish, National Trust)

To the west of the north end of Fargo Plantation, aligned from west-south-west to north-north-east along the top of a rounded rise, are the ploughed outlines of a ceremonial earthwork. It is 400 metres long and 60 metres wide. The banks survived until the site was brought under the plough during the Second World War. That said, external ditches can still be traced on aerial photographs.

There is a slight difference in alignment from that of the main Cursus, which follows more of a west-east line. This difference may be as a result of difficulties in establishing the mathematics of monuments aligned on solar appearance points. A cross-bank halfway along, with a ditch on its western side, may match the similar bank across the west end of the main Cursus. In both cases the internal banks are set from true north to south – as distinct from grid north on our maps – and fail to make right angles to their earthworks. The significance of that fact is that sunrise or sunset projections from the external earthworks may have been co-ordinated with the position of the sun at noon.

The shortness of the Lesser Cursus may be an indication that its eastern end was never completed, perhaps because the monument was then superseded by the building of the main Cursus. It may be significant that unlike the Cursus, the Lesser Cursus was brought into cultivation during Iron Age and Romano-British times, as part of an area of Celtic fields. This lack of respect indicates that it had already ceased to be a feature of the landscape.

Military Railway
(SU 099 392 to 230 393: War relics, several parishes, numerous owners)

A light railway, laid with standard-gauge track, linked the major Army infrastructure on both sides of Stonehenge during the First World War. To the south-west of the stones it had a cul-de-sac branch from the barrows north of Longbarrow Crossroads to huts and other buildings beside Stonehenge Aerodrome. Other branches led to Lake Down Aerodrome, Fargo Hangars, the Balloon School and Rollestone Camp, Countess Camp and Bulford Camp.

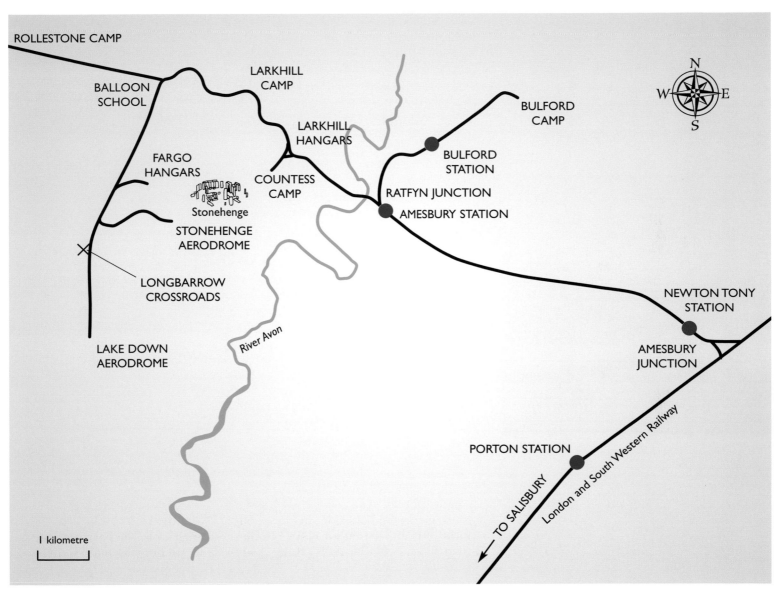

Stonehenge Military Railway, at its full extent, between 1916 and 1921.

The central section passed through Larkhill Camp, beside Larkhill Hangars, to Ratfyn Junction and Amesbury Station beside the River Avon. From here it ran to Newton Tony Station and then joined the main line of the London and South Western Railway. These double sets of points, known as Amesbury Junction, were between former Porton Station and the present Grateley Station.

The line from Amesbury Junction to Amesbury Station was built in 1901 and that to Bulford Camp was added in 1906. The lengths to Larkhill and beyond were added in 1915 and 1916. By 1922 these were disused and dismantling had started.

Traces of the line can still be seen in many places, and this has led to some confusion, such as where it was superimposed on the archaeology. This is certainly the case at Longbarrow Crossroads where it passed between the long barrow and nearby round barrows.

Monarch of the Plain
(SU 111 428: Round barrow, Amesbury parish, National Trust)

Although really one of the Cursus Barrows, this big mound effectively stands alone, having its own name and being separated from its contemporaries by the trees of Fargo Plantation. Its flat-topped mound is 25 metres in diameter, surrounded by a sloping berm 5 metres wide, and then a ditch 4 metres wide. The top is 3.5 metres high.

Monarch of the Plain bell barrow is separated from the rest of the Cursus Barrows by Fargo Plantation.

The Monarch of the Plain, known to archaeologists as Amesbury bell barrow No. 55, was an Anglo-Saxon boundary marker, that marked a change of course in its western parish boundary, between Fargo Plantation and Winterbourne Stoke Down. North-westwards this heads for Winterbourne Stoke bell barrow No. 48. To the south-west the boundary is in alignment with the linear barrow group at Longbarrow Crossroads.

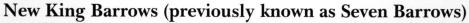

New King Barrows (previously known as Seven Barrows)
(SU 135 423: Barrow cemetery, Amesbury parish, National Trust)

The line of seven prominent barrows along the skyline east of Stonehenge Bottom is clearly visible from the stones, which stand 1,150 metres to the west. These barrows were formerly known as Seven Barrows. By 1985, when the

The view of New King Barrows from the west, on the ridge above Stonehenge Bottom.

Closer view of New King Barrows from the west, above Stonehenge Bottom.

New King Barrows, at the southern end of the ridge, seen from the south-west.

10-acre strip containing the mounds was bought by the National trust, they were almost completely obscured by dense scrub.

Since then, clearance of most of the bushes and trees has restored the King Barrow ridge as a line of little green hills, although they should be imagined in gleaming white chalk for contemporary effect. Even then, however, there would have been streaks of brown soil as will be explained below. New King Barrows, as a linear cemetery, stops to allow the Avenue to pass through a slight dip in the ridge. The Bronze Age burial-ground then resumes, as what we know as Old King Barrows, on the other side of the processional way.

Starting from the main road, heading northwards from beside thatched Stonehenge Cottage, the line comprises Amesbury bowl barrows Nos. 26, 27, 28, 29 and 30, followed by bell barrows Nos. 31 and 32. The bowl barrows are similar in size, being between 30 and 36 metres in diameter, and 3 to 4 metres in height. The two bell barrows are 42 metres in diameter and about 3 metres high.

There were another four Bronze Age mounds, since ploughed out, in the flat pasture to the west of New King Barrows. Slightly further away, above the cutting carrying the A303, the remains of Amesbury bowl barrow No. 39 was excavated by William Cunnington in 1805 and re-excavated by Paul Ashbee (born 1918) in 1960. The latter was able to extract burnt samples of bone and

The northern line of New King Barrows, still partly screened by summer leaves, viewed from the north-west.

wood from a mortuary pyre dating from between 1760 and 1580BC. Cunnington had found grave goods of amber and shale beads plus a shale button. There were pieces of a globular urn in the silt of the ditch.

The construction material for the mound included numerous sherds of early Neolithic Peterborough and Grooved ware, as well as animal bones and worked flints, which all dated from the previous period in the farming of this landscape. Such midden-like contents are by no means unusual and indicate that such mounds generally comprise loose material gathered from the surrounding fields rather than virgin chalk.

Normanton Down Barrows
(SU 115 413 to 124 412: Barrow cemetery, Wilsford cum Lake parish, private ownership)

Forming the best of the Wiltshire barrow groups, the mounds on Normanton Down have a clear view of Stonehenge and are passed by the byway south-westwards across the chalklands from Stonehenge to Lake Down and the A360 at Druids Lodge. Paul Ashbee protested in his study of *The Bronze Age Round Barrow in Britain*, in 1960, that ploughing, to their edges or worse, had razed 'the great barrow cemeteries around Stonehenge' in 'a process culminating in the dismal holocaust of Normanton.' For all that, they are still strikingly visible, forming the southern skyline of the central core of the World Heritage Site. They include sophisticated Wessex Culture mound shapes, sometimes in multiple forms, that Leslie Grinsell dubbed as 'fancy barrows' in 1953.

Bronze Age mounds were laid out along the low ridge, either side of Neolithic long barrow No. 13, and were aligned south-west to north-east, some 20 metres long and 1 metre high. Across to the south-west, touching the east side of the byway but almost left alone by later archaeology, is a second long barrow, 38 metres long and 2 metres high. This is Wilsford cum Lake burial mound, No. 30, which covered four skeletons that had been laid on the original ground surface at the eastern end. The mound is aligned from west to east and was flanked by side ditches. To the south is a rectangular mortuary enclosure inside a ditch, which can also be placed in the Neolithic period.

The closest large mound to the green lane, on the east side, bowl barrow No. 5 is Bush Barrow which was excavated both by William Stukeley and William

The central line of Bronze Age round barrows stretching eastwards (top left) *across Normanton Down.*

Bush Barrow (top left) *as the backdrop with Stonehenge receiving another 15 minutes of fame in a news report from the snow during the public inquiry into the possibility of re-routing the A303, in February 2004.*

The hole in the centre of Bush Barrow (foreground) *left by the removal of its rich finds.*

Twin barrows (foreground) *and a bell barrow* (behind) *on the east side of Normanton Down.*

Cunnington. Described by twentieth-century field archaeologist Leslie Grinsell as 'the celebrated Bush Barrow' it is 3.3 metres high and covered one of the richest of early Bronze Age burials. Stukeley missed this, but Cunnington correctly surmised it lay a little deeper, and sent John Parker digging into a veritable seam of gold during their Sunday outing on 10 July 1808. With the first intimation of these riches spread across the ground from the decayed wooden pommel of a bronze dagger, he reported to his mentor, Sir Richard Colt Hoare, who was spending the summer in Bala, North Wales:

There are now a number of these minute gold rivets in the remainder of the wood which still adheres to the brass. When we first discovered these shining points of gold, we had no conception of their nature, otherwise we might perhaps have preserved thousands of them, but unfortunately John with his trowel had scattered them in every direction before I had examined them with a glass.

These minute pins, each a millimetre in length, had apparently been set Breton-fashion into a pattern of running chevrons. Two more daggers were found, sheathed in leather-lined wooden scabbards, also with traces of elaborate decoration. These weapons were almost sword-like in size, the largest having a blade 24 centimetres in length, which was originally about 35 centimetres long when hafted. There was also 'the mouldered remains of a shield'.

The clothed body of a 'tall and stout' 'princeling' – Paul Ashbee's word – wore a lozenge-shaped breastplate of sheet gold incised with four squares, the inner of which was sub-divided into nine squares. There was a matching sheet-gold hook for suspending the wooden dagger scabbard from his belt. Beside his head was a flanged bronze axe wrapped in cloth. His right-hand clasped a 'lance head' and reached towards a mace which was taken as being his sceptre of authority. The mace head, hafted into a wooden handle set with rings of bone, incorporated a Jurassic fossil from the Devon coast. This stromatoporoid specimen has been identified as *Amphipora ramosa*.

Bell barrow No. 8, 41 metres in diameter and 3 metres high, also contained rich remains. An incense cup, criss-crossed with lined decoration, accompanied a gold-plated shale button, gilt-edged amber beads, and a votive halberd of amber and gold. Three Wessex graves have produced such pendants, but apart from 'a brass weapon of 20 pounds weight, like a pole-axe' recorded by William Stukeley from nearby King Barrow, there is no record of a halberd being found in a barrow in this country. They occur, however, from cist burials in Scotland and Ireland.

Disc barrow No. 3, between the byway and the plantation, contained a cremation of a female with faience beads from Egypt, amber from Yorkshire, and Kimmeridge shale from Dorset. This barrow is 60 metres in diameter, as is disc barrow No. 4, on the east side of the byway. Disc barrow No. 14, near the long barrow, is 67 metres in diameter.

To the north-west of the long barrow, next to a saucer barrow, bowl barrow No. 9 is 2.5 metres high. This relatively small mound was notable for a skeleton that was accompanied by a beautiful grape cup and beads of amber, gold and shale, as well as fossils and an urn containing food for the afterlife. Such sheet-gold globular and fusiform beads (shaped like a spindle or cigar, tapering at both ends) are a Normanton speciality.

Twin bell barrow No. 17 has two mounds, one 2.5 metres high and the other 2.7 metres high, which are surrounded by shared berms and a single ditch. This is 38 metres across from north to south and 57 metres wide from east to west. Grave contents included a cremation with amber and shale beads and a bone hook from a leather belt.

The eastern mounds include a bell barrow, four bowl barrows, three disc barrows, a saucer barrow and a pond barrow. No excavation records of these survive.

On the south side of Normanton Down, 100 metres east of bowl barrow No. 31, Mrs F. de M. Vatcher excavated a rectangular mortuary enclosure in 1959. The ditched structure had been 36 metres long by 21 metres wide. With rounded ends, it was aligned from west-north-west to an opening between portal posts on the east-south-east side. There were no traces of human remains, but ox and goat or sheep bones were found, as well as a rim-sherd of a Mortlake-style Peterborough bowl. An antler pick dated the site to between 2663 and 2457BC.

The discovery of such a site shows the importance of the apparently empty ground between round barrows. This was degraded here, as with almost everywhere else in the vicinity of Stonehenge, by the deep ploughing that has become commonplace since the Second World War. There is potentially more to barrow cemeteries than their visual remains.

Normanton Gorse Barrows
(SU 111 416: Barrow cemetery, Wilsford cum Lake and Amesbury parishes, private ownership except for the bell barrow which is owned by the National Trust)

The barrows west of Normanton Down, towards the A303, include Nos. 1 and 33 of Wilsford cum Lake parish. The former was dug by William Cunnington in 1805. He found a skeleton, 'drinking cup', and antler picks as its central interment. The mound of a denuded bowl barrow, 15 metres in diameter and 0.38 metres high, it was re-excavated by Miss E.V.W. Field in 1960.

She found a multitude of other burials, both primary and secondary, including another skeleton and many Beaker fragments. Seven infant burials and the crouched skeleton of a young adult had been inserted into the northern side of the mound. Grave goods included various vessels and beakers, a pierced boar's tusk, and a piece of slate that had been carved to resemble a bronze axe. The beakers were a mixture of Wessex, Middle Rhine and European types.

Normanton Gorse, known as Furze Cover in 1838, was created for fox-hunting purposes by the Duke of Queensberry. Its hazel and birch scrub has preserved a small block of former pasture which includes a section of boundary earthwork, running from south to north, and Wilsford disc barrow No. 2 which also survives in reasonable condition.

The immense mound of Amesbury bell barrow No. 15, the biggest in sight of Stonehenge, seen from the south-east with a military helicopter passing by.

Bell barrow No. 15 from the north-east, looking towards Normanton Down (centre right) and Normanton Gorse (far right).

The view from the top of bell barrow No. 15, looking south-eastwards across the next cluster of barrows on Normanton Down (centre, middle distance).

Bell barrow Amesbury 15, on National Trust land north of Normanton Gorse, is one of the biggest and best preserved mounds of its kind in the country. It comes with the perfect antiquarian credentials, being described by Sir Richard Colt Hoare as 'the most beautiful bell barrow on the plains of Stonehenge.' Its size is a notch above that of any of its contemporaries, with an almost flat-topped mound 30 metres in diameter that rises until it is 5 metres high. It is surrounded by a gradually sloping berm 5 metres wide and a ditch that is also 5 metres across. The latter is 50 centimetres in depth.

The primary burial was an adult male, placed on an elm plank in a fashion more common in contemporary Bronze Age Yorkshire, accompanied by a grooved dagger in a wooden case and an 'ornamental drinking cup', which fit Beaker period conventions. Beside them were antler picks and the upright remains of three tall wooden poles which had been erected beside the burial, either as a memorial or to show the builders the height to which the mound had to be raised. This perfect specimen has since been given its own fence, outside the berm and ditch, and remains an oasis of chalk grassland amid arable agriculture.

Old King Barrows
(SU 136 428: Barrow cemetery, Amesbury parish, National Trust)

Although not as well preserved as New King Barrows, and also associated with other ploughed-out mounds, Old King Barrows once covered the northern part of the ridge from the Avenue to the eastern end of the Cursus. Sadly, only six barrows now survive. They are Amesbury bowl barrows Nos. 41, 33, 34, 35, 36 and 37. The contents of these 'large and flat old barrows', as William Stukeley described them, are unknown apart from a sketchy account of seventeenth-century investigations mentioned by John Aubrey.

Fenced as a square barrow, Amesbury burial mound No. 35 among Old King Barrows, was removed from cultivation once the National Trust acquired Countess Farm.

Road Network
(SU 099 414 to 153 420: Turnpike roads, several parishes, public highways)

The A303
Historically this road's course wandered into wide curves to avoid muddy sections of track in Stonehenge Bottom. There is no evidence for a direct route here, as the ancient course of the track from Stonehenge Road, north-westwards from Amesbury, lay to the north between the northern two mounds of

Stonehenge (top right) *in its triangle of highways, looking west across Stonehenge Bottom from the site of a round barrow* (bottom right) *beside the A303.*

Above: *The Stonehenge milestone, 80 miles from London and 2 miles from Amesbury.*

Top left: *The road beside the stones, passing between the Heel Stone (top right) and a turnpike milestone (bottom left), briefly tamed by a winter wonderland.*

Bottom left: *Stonehenge Cottages, built in 1936, south-facing beside the A303 on the King Barrows Ridge.*

Fargo Ammunition Compound (top) *is the biggest landmark, past or present, located near the northwest corner of the World Heritage Site.*

New King Barrows. It then continued generally north-westwards across both the Avenue and the Cursus before crossing Durrington Down. The branch to the west headed towards the Monarch of the Plain bell barrow and crossed Winterbourne Stoke Down. Designation of the present course of the A303, as an A-class road, came in the 1920s. It was later upgraded to trunk-road status and remains one of the country's key strategic routes. One day, many of us hope, it will be put into a tunnel.

The A360
Although an ancient ridgeway, the A360's present course dates from turnpiking the route from Salisbury to Devizes, in the early 1760s. Before that the track tended to splay across the hills beside areas of ridge-and-furrow arable fields. It heads northwards to the Bustard Inn and Salisbury Plain.

The A344
The course from Shrewton to Stonehenge Bottom via the Heel Stone, this is no older than the turnpiking of the 1760s. The closest milestone, facing the Heel Stone, reads 'LXXX [80] Miles from LONDON, II [2] from Amesbury.'

The Packway
This ancient ridgeway forms the northern side of the World Heritage Site, eastwards from Rollestone Camp to Larkhill. The latter includes Horne Barracks,

Roberts Barracks and the Royal School of Artillery. Between Rollestone and Larkhill, inside the World Heritage Site, the bunkers of Fargo Ammunition Compound comprise one of the biggest explosives stores in Europe.

The Stones
(SU 123 422: Henge monument and stone circles, Amesbury parish, English Heritage)

After Neolithic farmers cleared the scrub and forests from the easily worked chalk soils of Salisbury Plain, Stonehenge was built on flat ground at 100 metres above sea level, with wide and open views in all directions for at least 1.2 kilometres. Visibility is substantially greater to the north, north-east and south-east. Skyline cemeteries, dating from the Bronze Age, etch the view to the east (New King Barrows), south (Normanton Down Barrows), south-west (Normanton Gorse Barrows) and north-west (Cursus Barrows). Another major cemetery lies just over the horizon to the west (Winterbourne Stoke Barrows).

Inside the bank and ditch earthwork of a henge monument, dating from 3000BC, Stonehenge comprises two concentric stone circles. The larger, outer circle is 30 metres in diameter and comprises sarsen stones from the Marlborough Downs that were brought to the site in about 2300BC. The inner circle of Preseli bluestones, brought from Wales, is 23 metres in diameter and dates from 2100BC. The interior of the monument is contemporary with these. Near the centre is the fallen Altar Stone, on the inside of two U-shaped settings. As with the circles, these are also duplicated – with inner bluestones and outer sarsens – the latter being formed of five great trilithons. The parallel sides of the central court open out to a width of 10 metres on the north-east side.

To the south-east, the Altar Stone is the largest of the Welsh stones. Its micaceous sandstone, also from Pembrokeshire, is 5 metres long by 1 metre wide and 50 millimetres thick. What makes Stonehenge unique, apart from the distance its stones were brought – by sea or river and rope-hauled on timber rollers across the hills – is that it is the only British prehistoric monument with mortises, tenons and toggle joints. The latter, dovetailing the 1 metre wide curving lintels into each other, were essential to its lasting stability.

The axis of the monument, from its central court, is towards the summer solstice sunrise and winter solstice sunset, although there are indications that earlier

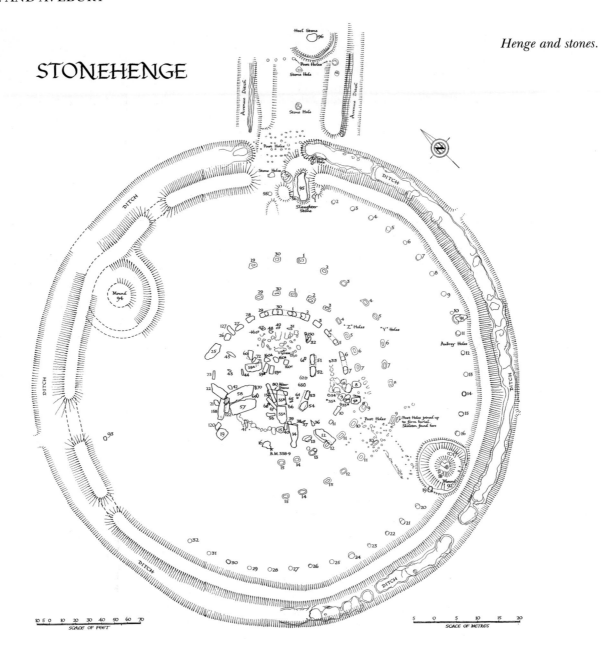

STONEHENGE

Henge and stones.

cosmological associations were dominated by an interest in the moon rather than the sun. Unravelling what we now know about the stones has been a long process, as the story of nearly a millennium of recorded history has been unfolded.

Unlike Avebury, Stonehenge and its surrounding complex of monuments retained its sanctity during Iron Age and Romano-British times. It must be significant that those who created great expanses of Celtic fields, remains of which appear all around, avoided what was potentially prime agricultural land. Stonehenge long pre-dates the Druidic period, and has no known direct link with the Druids of antiquity – who arrived in Britain in about 500BC – but they respected the integrity of the monument and its environs. They may have claimed authorship and ownership of a magical landscape which was put under their guardianship. It is one of those cases where absence of evidence is not evidence of absence. Stonehenge continued to attract visitors, who regarded it with awe and interest long after its purpose was forgotten, long before convincing stabs at its date and makers were being made by antiquarians and archaeologists. Folklore filled the knowledge gap.

Stonehenge reclaimed by the people for the midsummer solstice, 21 June 2004.

The Henge ditch (centre) *and south-east station stone* (top right) *seen from the east.*

The north-west station stone (top left) *and the Henge bank from the approach to the stones.*

Stonehenge as a ruin, in one of the rarest and most interesting of old prints, by French traveller L. Simond in 1811.

" Stonehenge."
Sun rising on th
longest day.

Edwardian postcard of the propped stones with a gathering of bicycles and carriages as the sun rises over the Heel Stone on the longest day.

Midwinter view of Stonehenge and the setting sun, in the south-west, as seen from the Heel Stone.

Stonehenge restored, in its subway mural, showing the stones from the north-east as they would have looked when complete.

A gap between bluestone pillars (centre), looking south-eastwards to a pylon in the mist, in a suitably icy view towards midwinter sunrise. The snow reveals the broad tooling on the surface of Sarsen No. 59 (foreground).

Stonehenge entered English literature in the twelfth-century chronicles of Henry of Huntingdon (1084–1155). He wrote descriptively of 'stones of wondrous size' being 'raised in the manner of doorways, in such a manner that door seems superimposed upon door, yet nobody knows how or why.' What makes this aspect of the monument remarkable, John Fowles reminds us in *The Enigma of Stonehenge*, is that 'Stonehenge is a ring not merely of doors, but of open doors.' They invite access and give all-round vision, perhaps so that those outside can look from this world into the next, and so that those privileged to step into the great secret within still remain in touch with the reality around them.

Henry had to resort to magic to explain how the stones were erected. In this the very name of Stonehenge contributed its own image, implying that the stones are hanging from the sky – or were built as a gibbet – because the root word 'hengen' was Old English for the gallows. Further fables followed with Geoffrey of Monmouth, Bishop of St Asaph (1100–54) in his *Historia Regum Britanniae*. Then came the poetry of Alexander Neckham (1157–1217). The earliest known illustration of the stones appears in a fourteenth-century illuminated manuscript housed at Corpus Christi College, Cambridge. This follows

Inside view of the sarsen trilithons, as seen from the south-west.

Military biplane and Army observation balloon over Stonehenge in 1915, with the sender of the postcard writing that 'much flying goes on around here'.

Stonehenge and its downland, including the Heel Stone (centre right) *and the closest bell barrow* (centre left), *seen from the east on King Barrows Ridge.*

The inner view from the south-east during restoration of the stones in the 1920s.

Colonel William Hawley's excavations, with the Henge ditch and bank exposed (bottom left). *Aubrey Holes are visible along with an archaeological spoil heap and huts behind the stones. The scene is viewed from the east in 1924.*

Geoffrey's chronology and places the building of Stonehenge at AD483, in the post-Roman period of legendary King Arthur. The caption reads 'Stonehenge near Amesbury situated in England. This year Merlin brought the Giant's Dance by art not force from Ireland to Stonehenge.'

Philip Herbert, 4th Earl of Pembroke (1584–1650), told John Aubrey that 'the central monolith' from Stonehenge had been carried off to the royal court at St James', Westminster. It may have been its socket, 2 metres deep, that William Cunnington discovered 'close to the altar' – the so-called Altar Stone – in 1801.

Court favourite George Villiers, 1st Duke of Buckingham (1592–1628) excavated Stonehenge and a barrow – 'or more than one' – in 1620 when King James I was staying at Wilton House. This dig, according to Aubrey, 'was the cause of the falling down or recumbency of the great stone there' – being Sarsen No. 56, which was 6.4 metres in length. It did not quite fall, however, as it came to rest on Bluestone No. 68.

The architect Inigo Jones (1573–1652) found, or was given, an incense burner and a lead tablet inscribed with unreadable vulgate Greek which was declared to be Druidic. Jones' *Stonehenge Restored to the Druids*, written in 1620, was published in 1655. The stones would never again be completely free from the Druidic myth, but at least he reclaimed the monument for the prehistoric British, from the competing claims of the Roman world. The Romans had been at the stones but only as visitors.

William Stukeley employed Richard Haynes – 'an old man of Amesbury' – to dig for him in the rabbit holes at Stonehenge. Haynes 'found some little worn-out Roman coins' but Stukeley thought he had planted them there in expectation of a reward. Ownership of Stonehenge, between 1639 and 1724, passed from Sir Lawrence Washington to Lord Ferrars, in 1655, and then to Revd W. Hayward.

Antiquarian interest continued apace. The first book to be devoted to Stonehenge, entitled *A Fool's Bolt soon shott at Stonage*, was written by Revd

Colonel Hawley in his trench through the Henge bank, in 1923, looking northwards to the Heel Stone.

Robert Gay of Nettlecombe Court, Somerset, in the 1660s. It did not appear in print, however, until the 1725 when it was published anonymously in *Peter Langtoft's Chronicle*. I reprinted it in my *Stonehenge Antiquaries* in 1986, after John Fowles and I identified Gay as the author from a note to John Aubrey from Revd Andrew Paschall of Chedzoy, near Bridgwater, which we had come across whilst editing Aubrey's contemporary account of *Monumenta Britannica*. In the reprint we added Robert Gay's signature from the 1669 Nettlecombe parish register. That year he recorded three burials. They were the last entries he made.

Daniel Defoe, in 1724, recorded the legend that these are countless stones. He gave the story of a baker, with a basket of bread, who placed a loaf on each stone 'and yet could never make out the same number twice.' Dr John Smith, in 1771, was the first to record that sunrise on the longest day makes its appearance over the Heel Stone. Bath architect John Wood, writing in 1747, records that his surveys of Stonehenge and Stanton Drew were both disrupted by severe thunderstorms which local people blamed on his activities. The learned were flocking to the stones. Dr Samuel Johnson wrote to Mrs Thrale in 1783:

Salisbury Cathedral and its neighbour Stonehenge are two eminent monuments of art and rudeness, and may show the first essay and the last perfection in architecture.

In the summer of 1755, the naturalist Gilbert White (1720–93), while curate of West Dean, near Salisbury, visited Stonehenge. He subsequently wrote, in letter 21 to Thomas Pennant in his *Natural History of Selborne*:

Another very unlikely spot is made use of by daws [jackdaws] *as a place to breed in, and that is Stonehenge. These birds deposit their nests in the interstices of the upright and impost stones of that amazing work of antiquity which circumstance alone speaks the prodigious height of the upright stones, that they should be tall enough to secure those nests from the annoyance of shepherd boys, who are always idling around that place.*

Jackdaws may still be seen nesting between the stones each year.

William George Maton told the Society of Antiquaries about the fall of a trilithon in 1797. Stonehenge was surveyed by pupils of Sir John Soane, the architect of the Bank of England, in 1806.

Stonehenge excavated, its Aubrey Holes visible around the inside of the eastern Henge ditch (left), *and the Heel Stone access point* (bottom right) *in an aerial view from the north-east in 1925.*

Stonehenge from the west, in 1930, with the station stones on either side and the Heel Stone and the Avenue towards the road (top left).

Midsummer sunrise, coming over the horizon above the Heel Stone (just visible in the central shadows), *in a classic view from the stones.*

The stones in 1957, the year before Professor Richard Atkinson's restoration, which transformed this view from the south-west.

The first Sir Edmund Antrobus bought Stonehenge, along with Amesbury Abbey and West Amesbury Manor, in 1824. Sir Edmund Antrobus (1818–99), the third baronet, refused to place Stonehenge under the protection of the Ancient Monuments Preservation Act of 1882. He owned 10,000 acres of Salisbury Plain. The former Liberal MP for Wilton, Antrobus resented the implication that he might otherwise neglect the monument, and rejected the need for Government involvement. He denied that 'visitors or tramps' were damaging Stonehenge and said that 'the scribbling of names' was 'only on the moss, and did not injure the surface of the Stones.'

On inheriting the estate in 1899, Colonel Sir Edmund Antrobus (1848–1915) of the Grenadier Guards – the fourth baronet – offered Stonehenge for sale to the nation together with 1,200 acres of its surroundings. His agent, Mr Squarey, told the Chancellor of the Exchequer, Sir Montague Hicks-Beach, that Sir Edmund would accept £125,000 but insisted on retaining grazing and sporting rights. No deal was agreed. Squarey said that Sir Edmund might sell the Stones to an American millionaire and have them shipped across the Atlantic; Sir Montague retorted that he would send a regiment of soldiers to prevent it.

Then, on New Year's Eve in 1900, upright Sarsen No. 22 and lintel Sarsen No. 122 collapsed together in the final hours of the nineteenth century. The report in *The Times* on 3 January 1901 was interpreted by superstitious people as presaging the death of Queen Victoria which followed on 22 January 1901. Even the *San Francisco Chronicle* took up the story. George Borrow had recorded the tradition in *Lavengro*, in 1851, that 'whenever that stone, which English hands never raised, is by English hands thrown down, woe to the English race.' Latter-day Druids claimed that stones had fallen at Stonehenge shortly before the deaths of Edward I, Edward II, James II, Queen Anne, George II, George IV and William IV.

Fears of further falls resulted in props and supports being placed against several stones in May 1901. The monument was fenced off – with barbed wire – for the first time in recorded history. Professor William Gowland (1842–1922) undertook safety measures in the autumn. Leaning precariously since before 1550, Sarsen No. 56 of the Great Trilithon was re-erected, after it had been parted from Bluestone No. 68 on which it rested.

The uprights of the Great Trilithon are the two biggest stones in the monument. One upright is 9 metres long, and the other 7.6 metres in length.

Stonehenge restored, seen from the east in 1972, when the stones were still accessible to the public.

They were buried to different depths in order to achieve equal height at 6.4 metres.

In the process Gowland accumulated evidence of the ways in which the stones had been dressed and raised. An international expert in metallurgy, he suggested the late Neolithic period as the material time, and advanced the date of 1800BC.

Sir Edmund imposed a shilling-a-head charge for visitors to the stones and said this was necessary to recoup the cost of what was described as 'the unsightly fence' and to pay the wages of two custodians. Professor Flinders Petrie, the Egyptologist, protested at the desecration of the monument. Sir Edmund again offered the monument to the nation, cutting the price to £50,000, but this was still dismissed as exorbitant. Mr Justice Farwell rejected a High Court application to restore the historic custom of free public access to the stones. He ruled that 'there cannot be a *prima facie* right for the public to go to a place where the public have no right to be.'

In 1901, Sir Norman Lockyer (1836–1920) published his theory on the orientation of Stonehenge, stating that its axis had been aligned upon the midsummer sunrise of the longest day, 21 June. This is as far to the north-east that the sun appears, pointing down the Avenue, but Lockyer's attempt at setting the bearing of the azimuth with precision (49 degrees, 34 minutes, 18 seconds east of true north) has since been questioned. Our sunrise moves in a 40,000-year cycle – the obliquity of the ecliptic – and has continued to drift eastwards since Stonehenge was built. For the midsummer sunrise to have taken place on the Stonehenge axis the value of the obliquity has to be 23 degrees, 54 minutes, 30 seconds. This gives a date of 1840BC. Sunrise to Lockyer was the first sun-beam breaking across the horizon, whereas to many observers it is half the sun's disc, and some people make a case for having the whole star in sight. It may be impossible to ever know which it was for the ancients.

To the Honourable John Abercromby, later the fifth and final Baron Abercromby (1841–1924), a much more important moment was midwinter sunset in the south-west – on 21 December – after which the dying of the light is reversed and the sun experiences its annual rebirth. That is at the opposite end of the Stonehenge axis. Abercromby noted that on the shortest day the sun sets to the left of the tallest stone, Sarsen No. 56, in what would have been the gap in the trilithon formed by it and fallen Sarsen No. 55.

Stonehenge, from the south-west, with an artist at work.

Sarsen No. 56 (centre) *and its tenon* (top) *viewed from the south-west.*

The megalithic monuments at Stanton Drew, Somerset, provide a similar calendar and calculator for the two crucial dates in the earth's year. Both have their importance in terms of harvest and planting, in cropping and hoarding, and are celebrated by festivities in cultures across the globe.

The term Beaker – of uncertain origin, as it may be from Old Norse, Middle English, vulgar Latin or even Greek – was coined by Abercromby. The author of the definitive study on *Bronze Age Pottery*, in 1912, he introduced Beaker to supersede Colt Hoare's 'drinking cup' usage. He considered that kingship in the Wessex Culture was a matriarchy and passed along the female line.

Stonehenge and its triangle of ground between the roads was put up for auction, in Salisbury, after the death of Sir Edmund Antrobus in 1915. It was bought for £6,600 by barrister Cecil Chubb (1876–1934) of Bapton Manor, Codford, Wiltshire, who retired to Rothwell Dene, West Overcliff Drive, Bournemouth. He proceeded to present Stonehenge to the nation, in 1918, and handed over its deeds inside the stones to Sir Alfred Mond, representing His Majesty's Office of Works. Chubb was rewarded with a baronetcy – being created Sir Cecil Herbert Edward Chubb of Stonehenge – in 1919.

Above: *Enigmatic Sarsen No. 10 (foreground), for some reason chosen to be half height, with Sarsen No. 56 towering behind, as seen from the south.*

Top left: *Stonehenge from the air, seen from the south towards the end of the millennium, before the extension of the pathway via the Heel Stone (top right).*

Bottom left: *Stonehenge viewed from the Heel Stone, showing the entrance with the recumbent Slaughter Stone (foreground), in a view southwards.*

The first major effort at reconstructing Stonehenge began in September 1919 under the auspices of the Society of Antiquaries. The aim was to push the remainder of the leaning stones back to the vertical, by use of screw-jacks, and then embed them in concrete. This work, superintended by Mr Griffiths as foreman of the Office of Works, was under the general command of Lieutenant-Colonel William Hawley and his helper R.S. Newall. Work started on 'raising and restoring' stones No. 29, 30, 16 and 7. It was brought to fruition during 1920.

Hawley became hooked on Stonehenge and with just Newall, plus extra hands during university vacations, he proceeded from reconstruction work into a general excavation of the site and went on digging every year until the winter of 1926. By this time he had stripped more than half the site down to chalk bedrock and moved outwards along the Avenue to the roadside fence beside the Heel Stone. This was the contemporary entrance point and remained so until after the Second World War.

Despite the prodigious amount of soil stripping there was a dearth of pottery. Dr O.G.S. Crawford used to say that Hawley had 'a fixed aversion' to pottery. Richard Atkinson remarked:

Since in general excavators tend only to find what they are looking for, it is probable that a good deal of evidence of this kind may unwittingly have been overlooked.

Hawley confirmed the north-east opening of the henge into the Avenue, a gap of 10.6 metres, as the only known contemporary entrance into the monument. The gap in the bank had been obstructed by a mass of post-holes, around 50 in all, about 1.4 metres apart and 0.3 metres in diameter. They seemed to pre-date the Avenue. Inwards, in the gap between the ends of the henge ditch were two empty holes, which had apparently held bluestone entrance pillars. The henge earthwork around the monument must have pre-dated the Avenue as its original entrance had been much narrower – only 3 metres across – and had been widened on the east side by filling 7.6 metres of its ditch. Quarried chalk rubble, without traces of earth, was 1 metre in depth. Digging the chalk had been done with antler picks; Hawley found 80 of them.

Around the inside edge of the henge ditch, Colonel Hawley discovered what became a series of 56 pits, about 3 metres apart. Positioned around the circumference of a precise circle, 87.5 metres in diameter, they were named the

The outer sarsen trilithons from the north-east with the Slaughter Stone protruding through the snow (bottom left).

The inner horseshoe of bluestones (foreground) *at Stonehenge.*

Aubrey Holes as a tribute to John Aubrey who was the first to notice these depressions in the seventeenth century. He called them 'cavities'. Most that have been excavated contained cremation burials, although only a few of these were contemporary with the original hole digging. There were no grave goods apart from artefacts such as bone hairpins and 'fabricator' flints, which are thought to have been used as lighters, by sparking against nodules of iron pyrites.

Frank Stevens of Salisbury Museum reviewed evidence that the Aubrey Holes, originally, must have supported 'uprights' of wood or stone. Perhaps these had been 'broken up for road metal', as some suggested, but Stevens supported another theory:

> *A far more interesting suggestion has been made – that the foreign stones* [Welsh bluestones] *originally formed this outer circle as unwrought uprights, which later on were removed to their present position within the circle of sarsen trilithons and horseshoe, and that previous to their second erection they were dressed in the form we see today. Certainly their number corresponds to the suspected number of the Aubrey Holes.*

An outer trilithon, now standing alone, on the eastern side of the stones.

Footsteps in the snow, from the north-east, as nature put some magic into the stones.

The generally accepted current view is that the Aubrey Holes date from the first stage of the monument, from 3000BC, and held posts. When these were removed in about 2400BC the holes were reused for cremation burials. Their positions are now marked by white discs.

In the same circumference, lying flat in the grass, only Sarsen No. 95 remains of two gateway pillars into the monument. They stood – or lay – either side of the monument's axis. Tooled and dressed, with a pointed base and flat top, the survivor is known as the Slaughter Stone. It is 7 metres long by 2 metres wide and 1 metre thick. As it lacks a tenon it did not form part of a trilithon, unless all of the tenon had been chipped away by souvenir hunters – it was customary to take home a piece of stone – and the builders of the monument had possibly intended to cover rather than erect it.

The hole was the length of the stone, rather than being a socket, but turned out to be not quite long enough to bury it in its entirety. The stone rested on the chalk at either end, with a void of 25 centimetres underneath it, and was therefore just visible from the surface. Colonel Hawley was pleased but not

quite delighted to find a bottle of port underneath it. Sadly it was corked – to use the drinking term – and dated from William Cunnington's excavation in 1801.

Two other standing stones survive between the Aubrey Holes. Sarsen No. 91, the eastern station stone, fell against the inside of the henge-bank during the eighteenth century. It is 3 metres long. Sarsen No. 93, the western station stone, is smaller but stands upright to 1.3 metres and displays patches of tooling on its north and south sides. A slight mound, north-east of Sarsen No. 93, also lies between Aubrey Holes and was found by Colonel Hawley to contain a stone hole. Opposite, south-west of Sarsen No. 91, is a similar mound which also had a stone hole. This was recorded in the eighteenth century and has been proven by probing the ground.

Lines between both sets of stones and mounds are symmetrical in relation to the ground plan of the monument and transect the inner stones at 45 degrees. It is possible that the four station stones served as a calculator for marking the movement of the moon at midsummer, when it rises in the south-east and sets in the south-west, and at midwinter when its arc is from the north-east to the north-west. Holes and posts might have been connected with calculating the subtleties of its azimuth – its angle in relation to the northern horizon – which varies by 20 degrees over a regular cycle of 18.61 years.

Hawley's next discovery, in 1923, was an inner ring of Y Holes (55 metres in diameter) about 10 metres apart. Then, in 1924, came the Z Holes (35 metres in diameter) which are 3.5 metres apart. The latter circle is within the bounds of stones which have fallen. In number, both sets equal the number of outer sarsen uprights. All the holes that Hawley investigated were empty – being about 2 metres long in parallel with the sarsens and 1.3 metres wide – and varied in depth from 1 metre in the Y Holes to 1.2 metres in the Z Holes. There was a fragment of bluestone, perhaps symbolic, at the bottom of each and more pieces both of bluestone and sarsen at random in the filling. Later pottery, from the Iron Age onwards, was found in the holes and is thought to have been placed there when the holes were filled at a later date.

These pits seem to have been used for construction purposes. Props from the Z Holes could have supported stones that were being raised. Meanwhile these may have been held in position with ropes from the Y Holes. Various experiments have been made to raise stones on timber cradles. The absence of traces of chalk ramps ruled out that method of erection. Despite these conjectures, the present view expounded by Mike Pitts is that the holes date from 1600BC – towards the end of the monument's active life – and therefore had nothing to do with its construction.

Inside the stones, Colonel Hawley found that the first arrangement had been much more cluttered than was previously supposed, revealing two stumps and four empty sockets under the grass between Bluestones Nos. 33 and 34. Later excavation, by Professor Richard Atkinson (1920–94), uncovered five more stones and sockets between Bluestones Nos. 32 and 33, and evidence for eight between Bluestones Nos. 40 and 41. The original layout of the stones was extremely tight. The ring of bluestones had been almost touching.

Inside the north-eastern curve of bluestones, Hawley found a series of Q Holes – the letter deliberately conveying uncertainty – on the inner side of which Atkinson discovered counterpart R Holes. These dumb-bell shaped trenches turned out to have been bluestone holes. The shape of the stones had been left as pressure marks in the soft chalk and there were 'minute chips of dolerite embedded in some of these impressions.' The radial diameter of their curves was 26 metres for the Q Holes and 22.5 metres for the R Holes.

What Colonel Hawley called the 'Stonehenge layer' was the equivalent of scalpings, with chips of bluestone, flint and sarsen having formed an apparently ancient surface, though in reaching this conclusion he ignored pioneering work by Charles Darwin. *The Formation of Vegetable Mould through the Action of Worms with Observations on their Habits*, published in 1881, showed how objects dropped on the surface are gradually carried through the ground until they reach a layer of chalk or another obstruction. Richard Atkinson's excavations showed that even Hawley's 'scatter of chalk crumbs' – left on the surface at the site of his spoil heaps – had been swallowed by soil movement and were 55 millimetres below by the 1950s.

The 'Stonehenge layer' represented a gravel surround between the stones, which seems to have been logical enough both to present the monument at its best and provide walkable and wearable ground. It would be an impossibility for a single ground surface, however well and deliberately prepared, to have survived in use for the whole of the 700-year period the monument was in regular use.

Despite Hawley's interim conclusions, this layer may have had little or nothing to do with the dressing of the stones, as sarsen resists fracturing into pieces and flint is just about useless for tooling boulders. Hand-held flint hammer axes and rounded hammer stones, varying in weight between 1 and 6.5 pounds, were used for surface dressing but the main work had been done with sarsen stone mauls. Frank Stevens, the curator of Salisbury Museum, described those in his collection:

Mauls of compact sarsen weighing between 36 and 64 pounds. The broadest side of these was more or less flat, and when wielded by two or three men they were capable of giving a very effective blow. Their use would have been for breaking the rude blocks into more or less regular forms; and consolidating the rubble foundations. It is especially notable that few ground or polished stone implements were found among them.

The appropriately named E.H. Stone, an engineer, was a regular observer at the dig. He published *The Stones of Stonehenge* in 1924. Stone put theories to the test and arranged for a mason to experiment in the dressing of a sarsen stone. Provided with a stone maul from the excavation – also of sarsen, which is two and a half times harder than Aberdeen granite – he pounded away at a boulder. Contrary to expectations, it failed to flake or split, and the only way to make progress was to grind away. The mason could only reduce the stone by pounding the surface into sand and dust. He managed six cubic inches an hour. It was slower with the mortises as these had to be ground out. Tenons were even more demanding as everything else had to be removed from around them. Building the main part of Stonehenge required slow-motion scouring of three million cubic inches of surplus stone.

This prolonged abrasion, to take off an average of 50 millimetres from every surface, would have kept a team of 50 masons – working nine hours a day – busy every day for three years. The stones they used as tools weighed from half a pound through to 60 pounds. The only evidence for use of metal tools was a stain on the base of the Great Trilithon, caused by contact with a small bronze object, and an awl from the late Bronze Age, near the surface of the henge ditch.

The sarsen stones had been roughly dressed in situ on the Marlborough Downs before being moved to the monument in about 2300BC. To allow for adverse weather and other interruptions the minimum period required to prepare the sarsen stones is said to have been five years. This has been calculated from experiments and projections based on a 50-ton stone, using sledges and timber rollers, with ropes of cow-hair and leather. On level ground at least 100 men would be needed to do the hauling, with another 100 on hand to keep replacing the forward rollers, whilst also preventing the load from veering side-ways. Hills, with gradients of about 9 degrees, were another matter. Here an additional workforce of 350 labourers would have been needed.

An alternative would have been sliding – with or without the use of a sled – stones along a prepared surface, all the way from Marlborough, which would have allowed greater control of direction. Then oxen could have been used to do the principal hauling. Either method would have required considerable effort in terms of preparation, either in cutting and making rollers or creating a hard, smooth ground surface.

In theory a stone could arrive at Stonehenge overland from Marlborough in a month, and the team could then return with the empty sledge and rollers in four days. All that sounds too easy. Not least of their troubles would have been leveraging the chosen stone free of the ground on Fyfield Down and extracting it from the obstacle course of other boulders. At the other end, 200 men would have been needed to raise one of the outer stones.

Being more practical, allowing more time for difficulties during the various stages and labours of extraction, dressing, transportation, erection and finishing, sometime between 20 and 30 years is a more realistic projection of the minimum time that would have been needed to complete the stone circles and horseshoes. The total labour force may have been up to 1,000. As well as having to contend with the weather, the work programme may also been put on hold during crop-planting periods, harvesting and festivals.

The bluestones and sarsens of the inner circle date from a re-alignment of the monument on the midsummer sunrise and midwinter sunset around 2100BC. The sarsen horseshoe could not have been constructed after completion of the outer circle as the larger horseshoe stones would not have fitted through the outside ring and there would have been no room to extended ropes to pull the large stones into the vertical.

William Cunnington thought the bluestones of Stonehenge had come from somewhere beyond Frome, in Somerset, though not as far as Ireland – thereby dismissing the Merlin tradition – but it is remarkable that archaeologists and geologists took so long in finding their original location. Their identification with the Preseli mountains of western Wales had to await a visit to the monument by Dr Herbert Henry Thomas (1876–1935), Petrographer to His Majesty's Geological Survey, for the Department of Scientific and Industrial Research. He reported in the *Antiquaries' Journal* for 1924 'On the origin of the Foreign Stones of Stonehenge, proving a Pembrokeshire source'.

Weathered blocks of spotted dolerite and rhyolites, as columnar and smooth as those at Stonehenge, litter the exposed summit of Carn Menyn in Pembrokeshire. Questions immediately arose: why and how ancient man brought stones to the middle of Wiltshire. A compelling and convincing reason that was put forward was that the Preseli mountains may have been sacred to Neolithic people as their Finisterre – the end of land – where the sun went to sleep at night.

The eastern end of the mountains of northern Pembrokeshire lies 130 miles from Stonehenge in a straight line. This is closer to 230 miles in terms of any practical route. That has to be via Milford Haven, by boat up the Bristol

Channel – known to the Romans as Sabrina Fluva and as the Severn Sea until the eighteenth century – and into the Avon Gorge, before coming across country to the River Wylye and Wiltshire's River Avon. That is a common river name because 'avon' was the Celtic word for water.

It was also in 1924 that Gordon Childe (1892–1957) put forward his theory for dating 'the Beaker Folk' of the Bronze Age and their Wessex monuments to the period now generally regarded as between 2100 and 1500BC.

In 1927 the Prime Minister, Stanley Baldwin, launched a public appeal to buy 1,400 acres of downland around Stonehenge for the National Trust:

The solitude of Stonehenge should be restored, and precautions taken to ensure that our posterity will see it against the sky in the lonely majesty before which our ancestors have stood in awe throughout all our recorded history.

A total of £32,000 was raised. The National Trust, with the co-operation of the Office of Works and backing from Amesbury residents, set about removing a motley collection of buildings down in Stonehenge Bottom as well as the huts and hangars of the wartime aerodrome on flat ground to the west. Thomas Hardy (1840–1928), who immortalised Stonehenge in the climatic scene of *Tess of the d'Urbervilles*, had been suggesting since 1899 that 'a certain area, shall we say 2,000 acres' – which is now the size of the Stonehenge estate – 'must be bought as securing control of the surroundings of the monument.' He was concerned, however, that the stones were being exposed to the force of 'disastrous winds and rains' and urged that they should be protected 'by a belt of plantations'. Stonehenge, in the clear light of day, failed to fit Hardy's mood:

The size of the whole structure is considerably dwarfed to the eye by the openness of the place, as with all such erections, and a strong light detracts from its impressiveness. In the brilliant noonday sunshine, in which most visitors repair thither, and surrounded by bicycles and sandwich papers, the scene is not to my mind attractive, but garish and depressing. In dull, threatening weather, however, and in the dusk of the evening its charm is indescribable.

In 1929, R.S. Newall and Revd George Engleheart investigated fallen Bluestone No. 36, by digging a hole beside it and feeling underneath the stone. Their probing fingers found that there were two mortises. This established that the 2-metre long prism-profile stone had been chosen and dressed for a lintel. although subsequent weathering showed that it had later been reused as an upright.

Stonehenge's great contribution to the archaeological lexicon is the generic term 'henge' to cover circular ditched earthworks. This was first used by Sir Thomas Downing Kendrick (1895–1979) who did less of a service to his colleagues by reintroducing Druids into the Stonehenge story.

Professor Stuart Piggott (born 1910) carried out a reappraisal of Colt Hoare's collection of barrow finds, plus subsequent discoveries, and came up with the term Wessex Culture for the rich lifestyle of Britain's premier prehistoric province. He believed it had been created by immigrants from Armorica on the French western coast. Gordon Childe initially reacted by saying that the evidence of multiple parallels made equal sense in reverse – viz, that the Armorican Bronze Age had been exported from Wessex. Similarities in barrow contents and metallurgy coincided with conspicuous megalithic enthusiasm, particularly for stone rows. These cultures were mutually accessible along the much travelled Atlantic seaboard that links Galicia in Spain with Maes Howe in Orkney. Childe later conceded that the Armorican peninsula had first claim because of the relative paucity of battleaxes with burials. Such easily portable objects might be expected to travel.

The death of King George VI and the coronation of Queen Elizabeth II, in 1953, marked an end to austerity and rationing and gave the impetus to 'a rediscovery of Stonehenge'. The Ministry of Works, as guardians of the monument, was prepared to allow excavations on a scale second only to the scouring of the site by Colonel Hawley in a similar political climate after the First World War. The archaeologist who talked his way into securing the commission was 33-year-old Richard John Copland Atkinson. Ex-Sherborne School and a former assistant keeper at the Ashmolean Museum, Oxford, he had since drifted north and was at the time the lecturer in prehistory at the University of Edinburgh. Stonehenge relaunched his career.

In 1954, along the northern part of the henge ditch, Atkinson found a silt layer 2 metres in depth. The filling included two sarsen mauls which were used as tools in dressing the stones. Many of these were used as packing around the stumps. Chilmark stone, a buff limestone from near Tisbury, was also used to hold them in place. One of the remarkable features of Stonehenge is that nothing at the monument came from its immediate surroundings.

The excavations at Stonehenge culminated with the partial restoration of the monument in 1958 which produced the monument as we know it today. As a result the stones occupy settings that are not always precisely where the makers intended. Then the evolution of electronic calculators into computers spurred renewed interest in the potential cosmology of the monument. Gerald Hawkins, in *Stonehenge Decoded* in 1965, suggested that the Aubrey Holes could hold movable posts to mark the 56 years of the lunar eclipse cycle.

Easier to understand, he gave the positions from which the movements of the sun and moon can be plotted through the sky, with simple geometry. Using the two mounds and station stones forming a rectangle inside the henge monument, he described the following positions which can be observed by standing on the ground. Sarsen No. 93 north-east to Mound No. 94 gives midsummer sunrise. Sarsen No. 91 south-west to Mound No. 92 gives midwinter sunset. Sarsen No. 91 north-west to Mound No. 94 gives the high point of the moon in winter. Sarsen No. 91 west-north-west through the centre of the stones to Sarsen No. 93 gives the low point of the moon in winter. Stone No. 93 east-south-east through the centre of the stones to Sarsen No. 91 gives the high point of the moon in summer. Stone No. 93 south-east to Mound No. 92 gives the low point of the moon in summer.

C.A. Newham took astro-archaeology a stage further with *The Astronomical Significance of Stonehenge* in 1972. He provided an explanation for the puzzling half-size stone in the outer ring. Sarsen No. 11 is 3 metres high, shaped like the others and dressed flat on top. Newham pointed out that this possibly intentional shortness – it may simply have broken – brought the number of uprights in the sarsen ring to 29.5 stones. He counted it as half a stone to arrive at the 29.5 days of the lunar month. Taking the number of bluestones inside the trilithons as 19, he arrived at a close approximation of the 18.61 year cycle recorded by the Athenian astronomer Meton in 433BC. After that the moon's phases recur on the same day of the year. Newham's calculations required a rope and peg as well as British prior awareness of triangulation geometry attributed to Pythagoras of Samos in the sixth century BC.

An excavation by J.G. Evans, who was taking soil samples for the study of snails in 1978 to determine the ancient environmental conditions of the area, revealed incidentally a crouched inhumation in the ditch at Stonehenge, west of the entrance. The young adult wore a stone wrist-guard typical of an archer. His grave had been cut through a deposit of silt and was dated to the Bronze Age by the presence of three barbed-and-tanged flint arrowheads.

Richard Atkinson made much of the fact that Stonehenge is unique in prehistoric England in being constructed of dressed stones. They are known from elsewhere, such as Bryn Celli Ddu in Anglesey, Maes Howe in Orkney and at New Grange in Ireland, but these sites have few carved or partially-carved stones and largely comprise natural boulders and random rubble.

Atkinson believed that Stonehenge owed its origins to Mycenaean architects and made comparisons with the Lion Gate and squared blocks in the wall of the citadel at Mycenae. He made this the main theme of his book on *Stonehenge* and claimed the indistinct incised outline of a dagger on a trilithon in the monument was a Mycenaean dirk. Further investigation revealed a total of 25 axes on the outer face of Sarsen No. 4 (facing north-east) and fainter traces of a single dagger and 14 axes on No. Sarsen 53 (facing north-west). There are axes also on the outer faces of Sarsens Nos. 3, 4 and 5 and a possible earth goddess on Sarsen No. 57. Several other stones have residual carvings, probably of axes, as well as other graffiti of many kinds.

As well as appearing in quantity at Stonehenge, dagger and axe carvings occur relatively regularly on Bronze Age stones, from Dorset to Scotland. Paul Ashbee pointed out 'that the apparently Mycenaean hilt of the Stonehenge silhouette could almost equally well be a representation of a local dagger.' The supposed Mycenaean dating has since been kicked into touch by Colin Renfrew.

Being architectural, Stonehenge required a ground plan, to mark its outer diameter of almost precisely 100 Roman feet. This unit of measurement from the Mediterranean long pre-dated the emergence of the Romans. In other units, the diameter of the stones equates to 29.66 metres, 97.3 Imperial feet, 64.8 cubits, and 35.38 megalithic yards (which happens to coincide with both John Aubrey's pace and that of the present author at 2.75 Imperial feet). Pegged out on the ground, as they must have been to achieve architectural accuracy, the centres of the 26-ton stones around the inner edge of the circumference are 3.2 metres apart.

The height of the trilithons is some 4.5 metres and their name – meaning 'three stones' – dates back to the time of Geoffrey of Monmouth whose twelfth-century chronicle recorded the belief that they had been transported from Ireland by the magician Merlin for the court of King Arthur. In a way, truth is stranger than fiction, as the stones were indeed transported over huge distances but by phenomenal levels of human effort and communal commitment rather than supernatural ease.

Colin Renfrew, now Baron Renfrew (born 1937), as Professor of Archaeology at the University of Southampton played a leading part in applying the revised calibration of radiocarbon dating to the mysteries of Stonehenge. In 1968, in his paper on 'Wessex without Mycenae' he pointed out that the antler pick from a trilithon – dated in 1959 to between 1570 and 1870BC – had changed in date to between 2100 and 1900BC as amended in 1967 by Hans Suess' calibration curve. Those dates have since been superseded, being moved further back, to between 2545 and 2055BC.

Renfrew's recalibrated date still lay within the span of Bronze Age Wessex Culture finds but ruled out the direct Greek connection on which Richard Atkinson was still dining out, with lectures such as that at the Red House Museum, Christchurch, to which I cycled. Instead, sharing the date of 1900BC, it made Stonehenge contemporary with Helmsdorf burial mound in northern Germany. Far from being the product of an unidentified Mycenean architect, Stonehenge was complete before Greek civilisation began, and also pre-dated the Egyptian pyramids. Suess and Renfrew had drawn what the latter called 'a fault line' – a neat geological metaphor – across European prehistory.

These changes in date, being a curve rather than a straight line, rise with time. Earlier dates, starting with the megalith builders of the Neolithic period, were set back by 800 years. Here the finds from around 2500BC were newly placed at 3300BC. Once again the new chronology did for the Greeks, somewhat ironically, as the word megalith is Greek ('megas lithos') for big stone. Diffusionist orthodoxy, which saw culture as spreading out across Europe from a common hub, was consigned to the bin.

Current thinking is that the bank and ditch of the Stonehenge date from 3300BC. By 2600BC a wooden structure had possibly been constructed at its centre. From about 2500BC, when the bluestones were brought to the monument, through to 1500BC there was an ongoing process of arranging and rearranging the stones. That period is now regarded as the general span of Wessex Culture.

The astronomer Sir Fred Hoyle (1915–2001), writing *On Stonehenge* in 1977, pointed out that the diagonal of the rectangle of the station stones and their counterpart mounds (without stones) were aligned on moonrise turning points. Similar arrangements or possibilities have been claimed for Woodhenge and the Sanctuary at Avebury. Hoyle took the astronomical geometry a stage further by showing how the 56 positions of the Aubrey Holes could be used as a prehistoric analogue computer.

Geoffrey Wainwright (born 1937), English Heritage's retired chief archaeologist, continued to 'stay on the case' with regard to Stonehenge. He came on the flagship Today programme on Radio 4 in September 1996 to defend me from critics after I had picked up pieces of bluish rock, indistinguishable from Stonehenge bluestones, from the beach on Steep Holm in the middle of the Bristol Channel. As warden of the island, for a quarter of a century, I had unique but short opportunities to scour acres of normally underwater pebbles exposed the during the lowest tides we had ever seen. Unfortunately, although helped by island workers Chris Maslen and Jenny Smith and other visitors, we could gather only small specimens and the three pieces I sent for investigation turned out to be not quite right. Despite this, Geoff Wainwright said it was quite possible that a barge en route from Milford Haven to the Avon Gorge had been shipwrecked in our treacherous tide-race. This kind of danger would have been present throughout the voyage and particularly possible in the vicinity of island obstacles. As well as being open to Atlantic gales, the Bristol Channel experiences the second largest rise and fall of tides in the world, and a close encounter with Steep Holm might well have been a one-way experience.

Our problem was that against all evidence, logic and reason, some geologists and a vocal minority of amateur archaeologists still insist that the bluestones of Stonehenge arrived on Salisbury Plain by sliding across the southern extremity of the tundra during the last Ice Age despite there being no evidence of glaciation of Salisbury Plain and area and a complete lack of bluestone deposits in the valleys where they ought to have been found if such a scenario had taken place. Wainwright set about searching the Carn Menyn mountain range and found unrecorded standing stones and circles. Furthermore there were other quarried bluestones, left lying in the hills, cut and ready for transportation. 'Stonehenge may be more Welsh than we thought,' he told Julian Richards and a BBC camera crew as he stood beside a huge horizontal slab. 'You could take this stone to Stonehenge, set it up and you wouldn't be able to tell the difference.'

The single twentieth-century statement about Stonehenge on which such diverse minds as dating specialist Lord Renfrew and cosmic adventurer Fred Hoyle could concur came from Richard Atkinson. He saw Stonehenge as the product of a society that was at peace with its neighbours and itself. For so many hundreds of people to have persevered at such labours for so long required the stability of a power-base controlled by a settled and unchallenged dynasty. Political power must have been 'in the hands of a single man' although 'who he was, whether native-born or foreign, we shall never know.'

Speculating on possible purposes over the centuries during which the stones were in use we may envisage Stonehenge as a calendar that carried with it a public purpose, such as for ceremonies and festivities, when the community may have processed into the monument from the Avenue. They could have filled the area of the henge and looked through the gateways of the trilithons into the central court, which can be seen as both a religious and secular focal point. Here the leaders or priests might have conducted the business of public occasions, from assemblies and declarations through to personal rites of passage marking emergence into manhood, vows of allegiance and marriage, and ultimately the celebration of death.

I imagine the users, alive and dead, arriving with the sunrise and departing into the sunset. Such a setting may also have set the seal on disputes, trials, punishments and executions. The evidence on the ground is of three possible circles of participation. The leadership and current subjects of attention were inside the stones. The community stood or knelt inside the henge. Their ancestors looked on from the gleaming white barrows that circled the horizon.

Over the centuries the uses of the stones must have evolved during their functional occupation, just as the settings themselves were altered and the landscape itself was subject to change.

Now the world comes to the monument. Stonehenge has a unique hold on the national psyche and is a place that every Briton should visit at least once. It is also a masterpiece of human achievement that is shared with the remainder of the planet. Since the Second World War, starting with the Americans and the Europeans and now extending to huge numbers from the Far East, Stonehenge has gone international. To judge from the voices and visual clues, at times half its visitors have come via Heathrow, and unlike the natives they make the effort all year round.

Stonehenge was No. 19 in the nation's top 20 attractions for 2003 with 776,279 visitors. Blackpool pleasure beach came first, with 5,737,000, followed by the British Museum at 4,584,000. St Paul's Cathedral was bottom of the elite heap with a 710,975 score. Few of the visitors to Wiltshire venture further than Stonehenge and its car park.

Not for them the experience of seeing the dancing stones. The legend, first recorded by Geoffrey of Monmouth, is that Stonehenge represents people who danced on the Sabbath and were metamorphosed for the misdemeanour. R.S. Newall, who spent as long as anyone working at Stonehenge in the twentieth century, experienced this as an optical illusion in a summer heatwave. Standing in Spring Bottom, south of the Stonehenge Bowl, he saw Stonehenge shimmer off the ground in a mirage.

Vespasian's Camp
(SU 146 417: Hill-fort, Amesbury parish, private ownership)

An Iron Age single-banked hill-fort of 37 acres, crossed by Stonehenge Road, rises from a bend in the River Avon west of Amesbury. There is a second counter-scarp bank along the west side, outside the main bank and its ditch, and a lesser ditch on the inside of the main bank which provided additional material for its construction. The domed interior rises to 91 metres above sea level and the south side, immediately above the Avon, is 22 metres lower in terms of altitude. Fords used to cross the river beside the island at the south-west corner.

The entrance to the hill-fort, at the northern end, is high above the roadside cutting off the A303 a kilometre west from Countess roundabout. The former ground level was a gentle slope. Although it has been ploughed since before 1397, as part of the mediaeval open field system of Amesbury parish, Vespasian's Camp was laid out as wooded parkland for Amesbury House in 1738 by Charles Douglas, 3rd Duke of Queensberry (1698–1778). Until this time, because of the substantial earthworks, it was known as Walls Field.

Landscape architect Henry Flitcroft surveyed the original park, entirely on the east side of the river, in 1726. It covered 30 acres. Rejuvenation was being carried out by Charles Bridgeman, the royal gardener at the time of his death in 1738. He laid out the 'Pleasure Ground of walks and vistas' along the west bank of the Avon. The Chinese House was built over an arm of the river below the eastern rampart of Walls Field and Gay's Cave as a grotto in the escarpment to the south-west. This was named for the playwright John Gay who was befriended and supported by the Duke after his opera *Polly* had been suppressed.

The romantic name of Vespasian's Camp, for the Roman Emperor who as a soldier had conquered western Britain after the AD43 invasion, was coined by William Camden, the Elizabethan antiquary. The northern part of the fort was previously known as Great Walls, to distinguish it from Little Walls, comprising the much smaller end on Gallows Hill.

Houses have been built here, along Little Walls, but the main area north of Stonehenge Road has become almost impenetrable woodland. Two Bronze Age round barrows, one of which partially survives, were dug into during the re-cutting of woodland walks and rides in 1770.

The 3rd Duke of Queensberry was Lord Justice General for George III, from 1763, and the King and Queen visited him at Amesbury in 1778. It was on thanking them in London that the Duke tripped as he dismounted his carriage and ripped his leg. Gangrene set into the wound and he died on 22 October 1778.

During the widening of Stonehenge Road in 1964, an excavation was carried out on the adjoining western bank of the hill-fort. It had been constructed in two stages. The original rampart stood 3 metres high and had been left to form a thin layer of soil, about 30 millimetres thick, before being strengthened and heightened.

The mixture of chalk and soil that supported a palisade was interspersed with early Iron Age potsherds which indicated that the hill-fort was a settlement as well as a place of refuge. Though not directly related to other monuments in the World Heritage Site, apart from contemporary wide areas of Celtic fields, it shows continuity of occupation throughout the prehistoric period.

Wilsford Barrows
(SU 118 398: Barrow cemetery, Wilsford cum Lake parish, private ownership)

Lying on the spur between Wilsford Down and Lake Down, on the western slope of Spring Bottom, this Bronze Age barrow cemetery has been flattened by ploughing or covered by trees. The sophisticated mounds as drawn by Sir Richard Colt Hoare have been largely eradicated. Their rich mixture of types included nine bowl barrows, five disc barrows as well as a bell barrow, a pond barrow and a saucer barrow.

The layout of the cemetery is nuclear rather than linear. The best preserved mound, in the wood, is the bell barrow at 45 metres diameter and 3.3 metres height, which covered the skeleton of a tall man with the full warrior chieftain's accoutrements of a stone battleaxe, bronze axe, knife handle and stone for preparing wooden arrow shafts. There was also a bone musical instrument and a cauldron handle. Rich female-related finds came from multiple tumps (hillocks) inside the disc barrows which were between 45 metres and 60 metres in diameter.

Excavations by E. Greenfield in 1958, of four barrows opened in 1805, included bowl barrow No. 51 where William Cunnington found two 'drinking cups' – since lost – and the skeleton of a child. The mound was cut through by a circular pit. Although the barrow would normally be ascribed to the Bronze Age, this earlier pit contained quantities of freshly broken Neolithic pottery, and other sherds from this period were found in the ditch around the mound. The pottery made a study in itself, including early Neolithic rim parts, and Ebbsfleet, Mortlake and Fengate types of Peterborough ware. Grooved ware was also present.

In No. 52, an un-ditched bowl barrow where Cunnington had found burials, Greenfield confirmed the total as having been four. He also found fragments of Neolithic pottery scattered through much of the filling of these graves.

Bowl barrow No. 54 revealed a hole which Sir Richard Colt Hoare described, already disturbed, during his 1805 explorations. Despite these diggings the excavation in 1958 revealed a piece of skull, a flat bronze dagger with a handle held by three rivets, and a Preselite stone battle-axe from South Wales. Pieces from three Beakers were roughly contemporary with such a burial, but there was also a spread of early Neolithic and Peterborough wares from the pre-barrow surface and underlying ground.

Wilsford Down Earthworks
(SU 112 405: Linear boundaries; Wilsford cum Lake parish, private ownership)

Extensive boundary earthworks, apparently from the middle Bronze Age, include a well-preserved section of boundary bank and ditch across Wilsford Down, to the east of the western byway between Normanton Down and Lake

The best preserved length of Bronze Age bank (centre) *between Normanton Down and Lake Wood* (top).

Down. It runs north-eastwards, towards the Normanton Gorse cluster of barrows, downhill from Lake Wood to the valley floor.

Clearly visible from the byway to the west, this is one of the few prehistoric boundaries in the Stonehenge area that still acts as a boundary – between two fields – and can be seen from the ground as well as the air. There would have been many more until mediaeval ploughing flattened so much of the linear archaeology.

Another bank, only intermittently preserved, runs north-westwards from Lake Wood to Longbarrow Crossroads.

Wilsford Shaft
(SU 109 415: Shaft, Wilsford cum Lake parish, privately owned)

A supposed pond barrow 400 metres west of Normanton Gorse was excavated by Paul Ashbee in the hot summer of 1959. He soon found what became the Wilsford Shaft, far deeper than expected, and he did not stop digging until 1962.

By that time the original cone-shaped depression had turned into a pit 2 metres in diameter and 30 metres deep. Ancient finds, more than half-way down, included sherds of a barrel urn and an ox skull. Towards the bottom were pieces of a globular urn and a Kimmeridge shale ring. Near bedrock, at the base, lay bone pins, amber beads, and the waterlogged remains of several wooden tubs and the ropes with which they had been lowered. Radiocarbon dating placed the organic remains firmly in the Bronze Age between 1470 and 1290BC.

It might have been a failed attempt at reaching the aquifer, but Ashbee made comparisons with the pits of the Mediterranean lore and ritual for alcoholic libations and sacrificial blood offerings to the dead. These are recorded in the earliest classical literature. For example, Philostratus wrote 'The gods of the Underworld welcome trenches and ceremonies done in the hollow earth.'

Pausanius, in his guide to Sicyonia, mentioned a priest in Titane who carried out secret rites in four pits. Each of these was believed to contain one of the four winds.

The Neolithic long barrow beside Longbarrow Crossroads (top right) *is aligned from north-east* (left) *to south-west* (right).

Winterbourne Stoke Barrows
(SU 101 417: Barrow cemetery, Winterbourne Stoke parish, part National Trust)

Winterbourne Stoke No. 1, the biggest and earliest of the Stonehenge burial mounds, is the 73-metre long and 3-metre high monument that gives its name to Longbarrow Crossroads and was erected over the body of an exceedingly important person. A single skeleton of a male was its sole primary interment. The mound is aligned from north-east to south-west where its higher and broader end covered the burial. The alignment points towards the setting sun at the midwinter solstice.

The main line of mounds in this Bronze Age barrow cemetery follow the same alignment. Heading north-eastwards these are the following:

No. 3: Bowl barrow.

No. 4: Bell barrow, 54 metres diameter, 4 metres high. Cremation in a wooden chest with bronze fittings which also contained personal items, including a large grooved-bronze dagger, knife and bone tweezers. The box was covered with clay.

Cluster of smaller barrows to the west of the main line (top) *beside Longbarrow Crossroads.*

Perfectly preserved bell barrow, in a view south-westwards, towards the trees at Longbarrow Crossroads (centre).

No. 3a: Pond barrow, 20 metres diameter, partly overlapping the south side of the ditch of the previous mound.

No. 5: Bell barrow, 50 metres diameter, 3 metres high. Sir Richard Colt Hoare dubbed this 'King Barrow' from its well-heeled contents. The primary interment, a skeleton in a hollowed-out elm trunk, had impressive grave goods including two bronze grooved daggers, a bronze awl with bone handle, and a Breton-type five-handled jar. One of the daggers, with a box-wood handle, was in a richly ornamented sheath. There was also 'an article of ivory'. Above the coffin was a bunch of fossil-like twigs which were the remains of a funeral garland.

No. 6: Bowl barrow.

No. 13: Bowl barrow 25 metres diameter, 1.5 metres high. The primary burial, a skeleton, was accompanied by grave goods including a grape cup and beaver teeth.

No. 7: Bowl barrow.

No. 7a: Bowl barrow.

No. 8: Bowl barrow, grave goods including a Beaker.

No. 9: Bowl barrow.

No. 10: Bowl barrow.

No. 77: Pond barrow.

No. 22: Pond barrow.

To the west is a second line of barrows, parallel to the first:

No. 2: Bowl barrow.

No. 16: Bowl barrow.

No. 16a: Pond barrow.

The main line of Bronze Age barrows at Longbarrow Crossroads are owned by the National Trust.

Bell barrows of the Winterbourne Stoke group seen from the north-west.

No. 15: Disc barrow, 53 metres diameter, with three tumps. The central one contained female cremations with amber beads and two incense cups.

No. 14: Disc barrow.

No. 13: Bowl barrow, 2 metres high, over a skeleton with a secondary cremation urn inserted in the side. A late Neolithic stone mace-head was found in the mound material. Colt Hoare also found two *Rhynconella* fossils and a piece of stalactite from a cave in the Mendip Hills.

No. 11: Pond barrow, 30 metres diameter.

To the north-west of these, beside the A360, are a third cluster of mounds:

No. 17: Bowl barrow.

No. 18: Bowl barrow.

No. 19: Bowl barrow.

No. 20: Bowl barrow.

No. 21a: Saucer barrow, 30 metres diameter and 60 centimetres metres high, with an outer bank.

No. 21b: Saucer barrow, almost levelled.

As well as these barrows, there are the much slighter remains of probable middle Bronze Age circular huts, associated with enclosures and a boundary ditch which has been traced for more than 4 kilometres.

The plantation and main line of rounds barrows mark the western boundary of the National Trust estate, with the fence line having been moved to include them after adjoining landowner J.D. Olding gave up 1.75 acres of ground in 1957. The stone stump of a mediaeval wayside cross lies in the pine trees to the east of the long barrow.

Winterbourne Stoke bell barrows viewed from the south-west.

Wood Road

(SU 144 436: Aviation relics, Durrington parish, Ministry of Defence)

Memorial under the trees in Wood Road, Larkhill, on the site of Britain's first military aerodrome which was established by the Army in 1910.

The earliest surviving aviation-related buildings in Britain and Europe stand inside the World Heritage Site on the east side of Wood Road at Larkhill. To the north of them, beneath roadside trees, is a memorial stone to Britain's first military aerodrome, for what began as an Army Flying Corps. Tombs Road is to the west, across a strip of scrubland, with what are now officers' married quarters at Strangways.

Bristol stockbroker George White founded the British and Colonial Aeroplane Company at Filton in 1909. Established with £20,000 capital, it became the Bristol Aeroplane Company, and opened Flying Schools here at Larkhill and at Brooklands in Surrey. The original line of hangars remain intact, although under the buildings ave been given new roofs. A number of the main doors have been blocked in to create storerooms.

Britain's earliest aeroplane hangars, beside Wood Road at Larkhill, seen here from the south-west.

The Larkhill hangars, built in 1912, and viewed here from scrubland to the north-east.

Woodhenge
(SU 151 433: Sacred site, Durrington parish, English Heritage)

As with the Sanctuary at Avebury, Woodhenge was excavated by Captain Benjamin Howard Cunnington, a descendant of the Wiltshire antiquary, and his wife Maud. It was identified as a ploughed-out disc barrow until 1925 and the advent of archaeological aerial reconnaissance. Concentric rings of pits or post holes appeared as crop marks inside the dark ring left by a filled-in ditch. This earthwork was 85 metres in diameter with a ditch that had a flat bottom 6 metres across and 2.5 metres deep. As with Stonehenge, the opening causeway of this henge faces north-east, towards the rising sun on midsummer's day.

Inside, in 1926 and 1927, Benjamin and Maud Cunnington found that the dark smudges on the first photograph – taken by Wing Commander Gilbert Insall VC, MC (1894–1972) – were caused by a ring of 16 large post holes with sloping ramps. These slopes indicated that huge tree trunks – confirmed in 1949 as oak – had been put into place. There were also a couple of similar-sized stone holes at the centre of the south side, but the excavation on either side soon started to show that the monument was much more complicated than this.

Two pairs of small post holes at the entrance appear to have contained sighting poles, comparable with the station stones at Stonehenge, although set at right angles rather than forming a rectangle. The western pair, on ancient ground between the bank and the ditch, are aligned from east to west. The eastern pair, also on the original ground level, lay beside the ditch on the eastern side of the entrance causeway. This pair are aligned from north to south. The northern hole is in a direct line with the western pair. It is clear from these four markers that the significance of the southern mid-point of day and the northern mid-point of night, as well as those of average sunrise and sunset, were known and marked several millennia before the discovery of the magnetic compass.

Within the main ring, there were three rings of lesser post holes, with the inner one being an oval 12 metres long and 7 metres across. Outside the ring of big holes that had featured on the aerial photograph there were another two rings

Woodhenge discovered, from the air, being seen from the south in 1925 (ring and dark patches) in the corner of the arable field near the road junction beside the old course of the A345 (right).

The entrance to Woodhenge, seen from the north-east, is aligned towards sunrise at the midsummer solstice.

Post holes, with concrete markers, outside the henge bank (coarse grass) at Woodhenge.

of smaller posts. The outer circle of holes varies in diameter between 40 and 43 metres. Once again the main wood was oak, although there were lesser traces of pine and birch as well as a rather hesitant identification of hornbeam. The positions of these posts have been marked with concrete stumps.

Near the centre, the small cairn of flints towards the south-west side of the inner space, marks the one and only contemporary grave that the Cunningtons discovered inside the monument. This contained the dedication burial of a three-year-old child. The child may well have been killed as a sacrifice – its skull had been broken open.

Sir Thomas Kendrick, who became director of the British Museum, published his study of *The Druids* in 1927. He claimed Woodhenge as 'a Druidic grove of the La Tene period of the Iron Age.' Subsequent research has put it back to 2350 to 2000BC.

It is impossible to say for sure whether Woodhenge comprised a collection of tall, tooled posts or totem poles, or even unworked trunks with roots in the air in the style of the Sea Henge on the East Anglian coast, or something quite different to match our colonial expectations of a proper roofed rotunda that might have been discovered in darkest Africa. Such buildings are known from Cherokee Indian Territory in North America. Whichever it was, the absence of occupational rubbish indicates a religious or, at least a ceremonial, purpose. The likelihood is that this was a temple or other form of meeting place.

Had it been roofed, which is physically possible, the outer circles could have served as a veranda and the inner circle as an open-air courtyard. On the other hand, as with the Sanctuary at Avebury, the use of perhaps movable posts to plot solar, lunar or cosmic calendars would have required an open air layout.

Four burials have been discovered including a cremation from one of the two northern-most post holes and a crouched male skeleton in the eastern section of the ditch. Finds included a fine Bronze Age necked beaker and a battleaxe in pink granite, from the eastern side of Dartmoor, typical of the fine quality artefacts and tools that found their way to Stonehenge. They are still being discovered.